It is such a joy and a blessing to know Albert as a friend and brother in Christ. This incredible story is a moving and deeply personal witness to God's grace and the transforming power of God's Word. *Grace Will Lead Me Home* is a book not only of hope but of the power of God's Spirit that is available to all. It is a gripping and dynamic true story that gives all the glory to God. You will cringe, laugh, and rejoice as you read it. I recommend it to everyone.

~John Hall Brown, Jr.
Architect, Church Leader, Marriage Mentor

This is the story of life that came close to being destroyed; yet nothing could be destroyed beyond God's capacity to restore. This is the story of God's amazing grace and of the power of forgiveness to heal, not only an individual but whole communities. This story will help you to recognize God's amazing grace in your life that God might lead you home.

~The Rev. Dr. Laura Mendenhall
Senior Philanthropy Advisor, Texas Presbyterian Foundation
Past President, Columbia Theological Seminary

I was deeply moved by Albert Cheng's gripping story and challenged anew to 'go into all the world' with the Good News of Jesus Christ. Who could have foreseen the fruit that would come from Christians showing an English language film about an ancient Jewish rabbi to a Cambodian Buddhist in a refugee camp in Thailand? This is the transforming power of the Gospel!

~The Rev. Dr. Shun Chi Wang
Office of Asian Congregational Support
Presbyterian Church (U.S.A.)

Albert Cheng is a survivor of the brutal war and Khmer Rouge regime. His life is full of traumatic experiences. This book miraculously demonstrates the power of God that changes Albert's traumatized life into a living sacrifice to serve God by bringing hope to others.

~The Rev. Thysan Sam
Survivor of the Cambodian Killing Fields
Eliot Presbyterian Church, Lowell, MA

This is an amazing and compelling story! I'll never forget hearing Albert share his experiences on my radio program, Renewal. I'm delighted his story is in print!

~Dr. Gene A. Getz
Host and Teacher, Renewal Radio

Grace Will Lead Me Home is riveting testimony of the transforming love of God. Albert Cheng's story will inspire all who feel they have been taken captive by forces beyond their control.

~The Rev. Bruce Reyes-Chow
Moderator, 218th General Assembly
Presbyterian Church (U.S.A.)

When I met Albert Cheng in 2007 in Texas, he expressed profound appreciation for my music and the blessing it had been in his life. Now, I am the one who is blessed by his powerful testimony in *Grace Will Lead Me Home*.

~Robin Mark
Worship Leader, Songwriter, Author

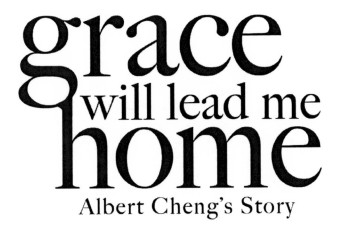

grace
will lead me
home

Albert Cheng's Story

Del Hayes

Del Hayes Press

Grace Will Lead Me Home
Albert Cheng's Story
Del Hayes

Copyright © 2010 by Del Hayes.
All rights reserved.

Published by Del Hayes Press.
1690 Estates Parkway, Allen, TX 75002, 972-727-3693
See www.delhayespress.com for information on bulk orders.

ISBN-10 0-9822706-3-1

ISBN-13 978-0-9822706-3-9

Library of Congress Control Number: 2010904010

Bible verses quoted are from the Revised Standard Version unless otherwise noted.

Front cover artwork courtesy of Herb Reed,
    www.herbreedwatercolors.com.
Cover design and graphic artwork courtesy of Elijah Farmer.
Photos of Albert Cheng and Del Hayes courtesy of Lindsay Horn,
    http://lindsayhorn.com.

Printed in the United States of America.

Del Hayes Press

Through many dangers, toils and snares
I have already come;
'Tis Grace has brought me safe thus far
and Grace will lead me home.

From *Amazing Grace*
by John Newton (1725-1807)

Contents

Acknowledgments

I must thank, first of all, Albert Cheng for having the courage to face once again memories he has spent thirty years trying to forget, and for his willingness to share his story of suffering and salvation. It is his hope, his prayer, that in so sharing he may in some way help others avoid such suffering, and find the joy of salvation that came from his ordeal.

I wish also to thank Mary Hodge, first for putting me on the path to write this book, but far more than that for her assistance every step of the way. Her contributions to the content, as well as her editing, organizational and promotional skills were invaluable in helping move the book along the path from inception to completion and success.

We are all grateful to the Reverend Paul Friesen for his insightful Foreword.

Special thanks are due to Herb Reed for his touching painting used for the front cover, and to Elijah Farmer for his masterful graphic arts skills. The talents of both are obvious in the front and back cover design, as well as in the interior graphics. Thanks also to Lindsay Horn for her professional photography skills applied to the photographs of Albert used in the book.

It is too easy to get caught up in writing a story, and let little details such as grammar and punctuation take a back seat. I am grateful to Kim Malcolm, Leanne McGinney and Mary Hodge for their dedicated editorial assistance. Little escaped their trained eyes, and any such problems that remain in the text are my responsibility alone.

I also want to thank all those who allowed me to interview them for background material. Last, and far from least, I want to thank my wife, Colleen, for her unfailing support during all the hours I spent on this project.

Map of Cambodia

Narrow line shows the approximate route taken by Albert in his first attempt to escape the Khmer Rouge. He was captured in the vicinity of Battambang.

The heavier line shows the approximate route taken by Albert and his 14 friends in their attempt to get to Thailand, after their escape from the Khmer Rouge near Battambang.

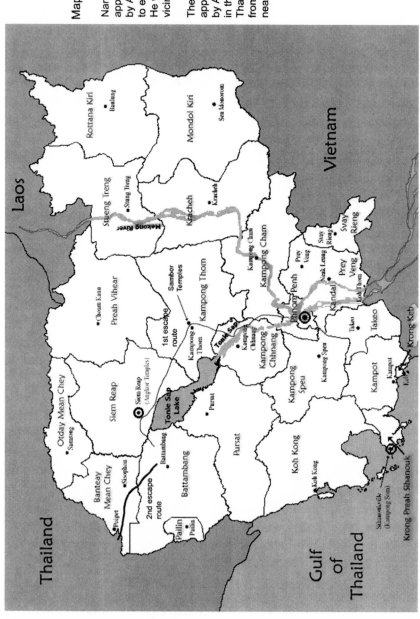

Foreword

Tragedy is about people: people we know, people with names, and families. Albert Cheng is one of those people. Perhaps, for you, Cambodia is a faraway country, too distant, too indistinct, and too different to know or to understand. Stories about real people from real places have a way of closing that distance.

A visit to the land where Albert grew up has many possibilities, with the ancient temple/city of Angkor Wat being the most well known and frequented attraction for tourists. Another option, more chilling but more apropos to this story of Albert Cheng, would be Tuol Sleng Museum—a school that was converted by the Khmer Rouge to the secret prison, known as S-21, that became infamous as a center for torture and executions. There are also the Killing Fields, those places that recall and depict the incomprehensible horrors of the Khmer Rouge. Historical essays and documentaries based on factual events, yet interpreted through the lenses of researchers and editors, assist us as we sort through the events, people and factors that contributed to that tragedy.

In this book you will read a story of grace in the midst of such tragedy. As Albert tells his story to Del the complexities and contradictions of life in Cambodia begin to unfold. *Grace Will Lead Me Home* takes us through the time and places of Cambodia's worst nightmare. It is a story of how Albert's life was shattered by the relentless determination of the Khmer Rouge to implement their insane utopian dream. Albert's story takes us back to the life he had before the Khmer Rouge, and seeks to reconstruct the historical events leading up to the Killing Fields. It includes unexplainable twists and turns of their rise to power and the tragic events that follow.

Grace Will Lead Me Home is a story of a spiritual journey, one that unfolds as Albert wrestles with his Buddhist faith and discovers a God he never knew. As Albert's four-year struggle to escape reaches a pinnacle, hope in the midst of despair is found. We are taken from a life devastated by years in captivity to his escape, to the refugee camp, and finally to America.

In this new land, encounters with Christians and their churches expose him to people who believe in a God they can not see. In an act of indescribable grace, this God appears to Albert and his spiritual eyes are opened to see the One Who has been with him every step of the way. Albert's story is one of God's amazing grace—grace that is available to all—grace that led Albert home, and grace that can lead you home.

The Reverend Paul Friesen
Regional Liaison for Laos, Cambodia, and Vietnam
Presbyterian Church (U.S.A.)

Preface

Is that a light? he wondered, uncertain if his mind was playing tricks on him. The jungle can do that. Its heavy canopy shields the sun by day, and creates new meaning to darkness, at night. It had become an isolation ward, a sensory deprivation chamber. How long had it been since they made their panic-stricken dash for freedom into the jungle? Weeks? Months? Nearly four years of brutal captivity in slave labor camps, of being little more than a mindless robot, had destroyed all normal sense of time.

Every day had been the same. What did Monday mean? What was Wednesday? There was only sun up, sun down. Sun up, sun down. Nothing else had meaning. Do as you are told. Wrap yourself in silence. Survive. Even if life often seemed less appealing than death, the body is created for life. So he had survived, even though life had become nothing but evil and darkness. But now he was seeing a light.

His mind could not assure him that what his eyes were seeing was real. He closed his eyes, shook his head, and looked again. Distant but distinct, the light was still there. He moved his head a little, and the light disappeared behind trees. Slowly, he moved his head back. It reappeared.

The light had to be real, and if real it could mean but one thing: he had survived to reach the border of Thailand. Reaching that light would mean that his escape from the horror of the last four years was finally complete. His voice subdued, always fearful of alerting the bands of soldiers that frequently roamed the area, he called to the others, pointing to the light.

In 1979, fifteen starving, scared, desperate young escapees from the "Killing Fields" of the Khmer Rouge huddled together in the darkness of the Cambodian jungle looking at a light, a beacon on a shore not much more distant than the length of a couple of football fields, perhaps less. Though the group is not yet aware of it, the light is a refugee camp run by the United Nations, just inside the Thailand side of the border with Cambodia. The field ahead of them is not free of trees, but more open than the jungle. It is all that now stands between them and freedom.

For unnumbered days they have slept on the jungle floor, living on insects, rats, cobras—anything that could be caught and eaten to help survive a few more hours—drinking sap and moisture collected from the leaves of vines and trees. Night after meaningless day they struggled against all odds, fighting their barefooted way through tall, tough grass and dense jungle growth, trying to stay alive, incapable of measuring progress toward a goal that they could only hope existed somewhere in front of them. Today's patch of jungle looked just like yesterday's, which would look just like tomorrow's.

Much of the time they had to sleep hidden in undergrowth by day, traveling at night, trying to avoid detection by the roaming bands of Khmer Rouge troops and bandits that constantly threatened them. On occasion, the clanking of canteens and ammo belts alerted them to an approaching patrol, forcing them to dive into the undergrowth, hiding until the threat had disappeared.

After all that, a shining light of freedom now beckons to them from across that field, across the invisible line that separated free Thailand from the prison that was their home country of Cambodia.

But not seen along that line are thousands of land mines, buried by the government of Thailand, ostensibly to guard against incursions by Khmer troops. Though it might not be publicly admitted, the mines were also intended to stem the flood of Cambodian refugees into Thailand, seeking safety. Also hidden in the undergrowth are sharply pointed, oft-times poisoned, bamboo "punji" stakes. Stepping on one of those mines, falling on those stakes, means severe injury or—much more likely—painful death. As if that were not sufficient, Thai troops are stationed along the border, with orders to shoot anything that might dare an attempt to cross that field, to cross the border.

They had barely escaped detection on several occasions by patrols of Khmer Rouge troops. The sound of distant gunfire as the group fought its way through the jungle was a constant reminder that certain death awaited them if they failed in their bid to escape and were captured. As they stare at the distant light, the group grows increasingly apprehensive, increasingly desperate, talking nervously, quietly, afraid the very sound of their voices will seal their fate. They feel paralyzed, each awaiting another to make the first move.

One of the fifteen, an emaciated, skeletal young Buddhist, looks across the field, aware of the ever-present danger of the Khmer Rouge behind him. Going back, staying put, are not options. But he is also aware that both the Thais and the Cambodians have mined the borders during the many years of conflicts between the two countries. He can only imagine what lies buried between him and that distant light.

"While I was a prisoner in one of the Khmer Rouge camps," he later recalled, "I once saw a large white crane flying free over the camp. I didn't dare let the tears fall that were welling up within me. To the Khmer Rouge, tears meant that you were dissatisfied with your life—and you would be severely beaten, or executed. But I watched that crane, and dreamed of being free like that, able to fly away from my hell on earth. I remembered that crane as I looked at the light. I thought, *If I can cross, I can be free. But if I die, at least I will die free.*"

Closing his mind to his fear, he leaves the group and bolts toward the light. Spurred out of their paralysis, the others quickly follow.

"It only took a moment before a big blast and flash of light made it obvious that one of us had stepped on a mine. I didn't look. It was dark. I could barely see. I couldn't help, anyway. I just kept running, trying to keep the light in front of me. The mine going off alerted the Thai soldiers, and they soon opened up on us with mortars and small arms," he related.

Thailand and Cambodia had been traditional enemies for centuries. But now, with Cambodia under control of the Khmer Rouge, relations between the two countries had deteriorated even more as refugees pouring into Thailand were threatening to overwhelm the government. The Thai troops weren't taking chances, and didn't particularly care who might have been approaching. At the sound of the first mine going off, they opened fire into the darkness.

"Bullets began whizzing all around me. I could hear them, zip, zip, whizzing through the leaves, thunking into trees. Sometimes they came so close I could feel the pressure, smell the heated air. Mines were blowing up around me, and mortars exploding. I heard screams in the darkness. 'Help me, help me.' But I knew I couldn't stop, couldn't help. I just ran toward the lights. I couldn't think. Dead? Alive? What did that mean? My mind was so numb from all that I had seen and suffered for the past years, dead or alive made little difference. I was blank to all that was happening around me, the explosions, the noise and screams, the gunfire. Then, at some point, I fell down."

The refugee camp had been set up by the United Nations Border Relief Operation, or UNBRO, with the permission of the Thai government but without its support. At the sound of the gunfire, and mines exploding, a group from the camp jumped in a truck and set out to try to find any who might have survived an attempt to cross the border.

"I just lay there. My mind was too numb from the years in the camps, and all that was exploding around me, to feel either dead or alive. Then someone grabbed my arm and lifted me up, helped me stand. They loaded me in the truck and we took off. In a few minutes, we were in the camp."

By whatever miracle, he was alive, safe at last in the UNBRO camp. After enduring captivity for most of the four years that Cambodia was under the Khmer Rouge, four years that ultimately saw nearly two million—perhaps many more, as there is no way of accurately knowing—of his fellow Cambodians die at the hands of their captors, he had survived.

Thirty years or so, later, a Presbyterian lay minister from Texas is standing before a group of Cambodian military officers at a base in Cambodia. Most, or more likely all, of the men facing him are life-long Buddhists. He has been witnessing to this group about a new God, and his new religion called Christianity. They have listened politely to his personal profession of faith, and his story of how the Spirit of God miraculously washed over him one night.

Stoic as the Buddha they worship, they have listened in silence as he has told them of how the love of this God washed his soul clean, driving out the demons that tore at his mind and soul for so many years. Now he has invited them to leave behind their old ways, their old culture, and walk in this new faith with him.

"If you want to accept this God, accept His Son Jesus who died to save us from our sins, you don't have to do anything—just raise your hand," he tells them.

One of the members of the group, dressed in the uniform of a high-ranking officer, stands and looks at the minister. He asks him a simple, but profound, question. Much will rest on the answer of the minister.

"If I follow this new God of yours, what do I do with this?" the officer challenges, pulling out from his shirt front a chain worn round his neck. On the chain is the emblem of the Golden Buddha. The room is silent, waiting for the minister to answer.

The minister hesitates, apprehensive and uncertain. He feels intimidated by the officer. No, it is more than that. He is frightened by this man. The minister has no uncertainty about his own faith, he has no doubts about his "new God," believing with all his heart that the Holy Spirit will provide the answer to this question. But he remains mute.

His hesitation, his nervousness, is noticed by the group, and some of them shift nervously in their chairs. The officer waits, holding the Golden Buddha in his hand, looking at the minister. Then another uniformed member stands, and addresses the officer.

"Sir, if you come to the Mekong River and want to cross, and there are two canoes, you would not put one foot in each canoe. You must choose one, or the other."

For several seconds the officer doesn't respond. Then he removes the Golden Buddha, and slowly raises his hand. As he does so, every other member of the group joins him, raising their hands.

These two vignettes, both described in detail in later chapters, are presented in brief form here to serve, in a sense, as the prologue and the epilogue. That is because the wretched young Buddhist who collapsed at the fence of the United Nations camp thirty years earlier was the same person as the Presbyterian lay minister standing facing the military group. His name is Albert Cheng.

And the officer? Now a friend of Albert's, he is a former Khmer Rouge officer, one who had been personally responsible for the deaths of hundreds of Cambodians—conceivably including members of Albert's own family. Albert had returned to Cambodia to share the Christian faith that had rescued him from the carnage of years of captivity under people like the commander.

He returned to his homeland not with an AK-47 seeking revenge but, through his new-found Lord and Savior, with enough love in his heart to do as Jesus bade him do: "Love your enemies, pray for those who persecute you."

Albert's story—his life—is an humble testimony to the love of God, and God's amazing grace.

Albert Cheng relates the story of his persecution under the Khmer Rouge, his miraculous escape to America and his conversion to Christianity, during one of the interview sessions with author, Del Hayes (right). (photo by Lindsay Horn)

Introduction

Return to your fortress, O prisoners of hope; even now I announce that I will restore twice as much to you.

Zechariah 9:12 (NIV)

This is a story of contradictions. Best symbolized by the picture on the cover of a white crane flying free, the contradictions are not so much in what is seen but in what is not seen. The story behind that picture is told in later chapters. It is a story of the worst in human nature, of the worst that man can do to his fellow man. But it is also a story of the best in human nature, of survival, of hope and inspiration. It is a story of salvation, of the lost being found. It is a story of God's saving grace.

Although the prologue to the story has roots stretching back to the 1860s, the story officially starts on January 10, 1955, in central Cambodia. On that day, a son was born to the Cheng Uy family. They named him Sophanarith.

Cambodians traditionally place their surname first; we would have referred to them as the Cheng family. Sophanarith, the newborn son, was the fifth in what was to become a family of nine brothers and sisters in the Cheng family. As he grew and came of age, he led a life he remembers as rather idyllic. But when he left his home to attend college in the capital city of Phnom Penh, events literally exploded around him that changed his life, nearly destroyed his life, but eventually came to transform his life. Those events also came to affect my life, in ways I could not have imagined in 1955.

January 10, 1955, was a Monday, on my side of the globe. I was attending college in my home town in Kansas and probably would have been in class, thinking about things that nineteen-year-old guys are prone to think about. But one thing I most certainly would not have been thinking about was what was going on that day in a town whose name I couldn't pronounce, in a country equally foreign to me on the back side of the globe.

One of the advantages of having traveled a fair distance down life's road is that you have a perspective that you cannot have as a young person. To have perspective, you have to have experienced life, and on January 10, 1955, I had not yet experienced much of my life. I certainly had not experienced it sufficiently to comprehend how events that were occurring that day half a world away from my small hometown would come to affect my life.

Four decades were to pass before the paths of a boy from the farms of Kansas and a boy from the jungles of Cambodia crossed, at the most unlikely of places—the playground of a church school in north central Texas. It is often said that God works in mysterious ways, His wonders to perform. That crossing of paths happened for the simple reason that Colleen, my wife, likes to play with two-year-olds.

At the time, in the mid-nineties, Colleen worked part-time at the school operated by our church, Canyon Creek Presbyterian, in the Dallas suburb of Richardson, Texas. One day, as was her usual custom, Colleen began to relate her day's activities to me after I arrived home from work. She wanted to tell me about the interesting man she was getting to know, who was now working as a custodian at the church. His name, she told me, was Albert Cheng.

"I can't understand him very well, but we have fun attempting to visit with each other. He likes to come out to the playground when we have the kids outside. He says he used to climb trees in the jungles of his home in Cambodia, and climbs them like a monkey. I've seen him scramble up on the church roof like he has a ladder. From what I understood him to say he was a prisoner of the Khmer Rouge, but finally escaped. He said he had to live off cobras while he was escaping through the jungles. I told him we had rattlesnakes on our farm when I was growing up. We laughed with each other while we compared notes on which snake was the most deadly."

I was vaguely aware of the story of the Khmer Rouge taking over Cambodia, and the horror of their "Killing Fields," but I had never paid much attention to any of it. I certainly never expected to meet someone who had survived such atrocities. Albert intrigued me. It seemed so incongruous that a person who appeared to be such an humble, gentle sort of man with a wry, quiet sense of humor could have endured and survived such horrific treatment. On the occasions that we might meet, I would greet him but we didn't visit much. Most of his visiting was with Colleen at the school, as they shared stories of their homelands and entertained the kids.

Several years passed, and the story might have remained at that point—that is, no story at all, at least for me—had not God's mysterious ways continued on their mysterious course. Not so long ago I was talking to our church librarian about a book I had just published. During our conversation I made a casual comment that, like tossing a pebble into a pond, spread its ripples far beyond anything I imagined at the time.

"The book I would really like to write is the story of Albert Cheng," I told her. "I can't imagine a more compelling story than all that he survived under the Khmer Rouge, eventually winding up working at a church in Texas, converting from Buddhism to Christianity, and now helping to bring his new faith—and healing—to his homeland."

I meant what I said. It is a compelling story and as a writer, I thought telling that story would be an interesting challenge. At the time, though, my comment was mostly hypothetical, simply conversational. I had more than enough to keep me busy, and didn't give much thought to actually undertaking the effort. But that was about to change.

Not long after making that comment, I saw Mary Hodge, who was collecting money for a church supper Colleen and I were attending. Mary had joined the church staff a couple of years after Albert was hired as custodian at our church. He had turned to Mary to read scriptures to him and support his quest for learning about this new religion of Christianity that surrounded him while he was busy being a custodian.

"I'd like to talk with you about Albert's book," she said, as she took my check. "Could you meet with me anytime soon to talk about it?"

Word had apparently gotten around that I had expressed an interest in writing a book about Albert. Mary and I arranged to meet and discuss the possibility. During that meeting we agreed that his is a story worth telling and that needs to be told. I expressed my concern that reopening those old emotional wounds might be harder on Albert than it would be worth, and wondered if we should subject him to it.

"Albert is so on fire with the Holy Spirit that he craves the opportunity to tell how the Lord worked, and continues to work, in his life," Mary assured me. "He feels he is finally emotionally ready to share his experiences. He knows that reliving those experiences, bringing back to the present what he has struggled for so long to forget, will be difficult and painful at times. But he wants to do what he can to help assure that nothing like the Killing Fields ever happens to his country—or anybody's country—again."

It soon became apparent that we were all being led to turn this overwhelming story into a book.

This, then, is the story of Cheng Sophanarith. Of course, by the time he had made it to America and came to work at our church he had long since Americanized his name. To us, he is our friend, Albert Cheng. (There is an interesting aside regarding his choice of the name, "Albert." Cambodian schools were often taught in French, and Albert said he had been impressed as a student by the French philosopher, Albert Camus. In lieu of anything better, he chose that name.)

The day came, then, when we gathered to begin interviewing Albert, to begin the task of getting his story told. As he sat in a rocking chair in our living room during our interview sessions, looking out the bay windows at our trees and the squirrels and birds flitting around, he poured out his life story. Usually, Mary Hodge and Colleen would join us for the sessions. I would occasionally ask the questions I had prepared, but mostly we all just sat and listened.

Sometimes he would smile at the birds on our feeders, or when the view of the trees and fields seen out our windows reminded him of some childhood memory. Other times he would hesitate in mid-sentence, a hard, pained look on his face as he struggled to keep back tears. But in a moment, he would look back at us, perhaps make an aside comment about what he had just been seeing in his mind, and we would continue on.

As we did so, I began to feel that I was experiencing something life-changing. I listened to stories of indescribable horror, of experiences that stretched the limits of human cruelty and endurance, told in his quiet, unassuming way. Later on, we laughed with him as he told of coming to a strange country where he knew not a soul and could not read so much as a street sign. He told of being afraid to ride a city bus because he had no way of knowing where it would take him or if he could ever find his way back.

But then, he began relating his experiences of struggling to find what he called "God with a capital G." There were moments when I wished for a video camera so I could include his reaction when telling of fighting his internal demons and of seeing the blinding light in his dreams of a Savior he had long been seeking. Waving his arms over his head in a big circle, a smile on his face, he would tell how the Spirit would just "whooooosh" over him, pouring into him, cleansing his soul, changing his life.

Although this book is about Albert Cheng it is, in a sense, the story of two sons. Both sons were born to Cambodian parents, one thirty years before the other, in villages scarcely forty miles apart. Both had parents who were better off than most others they knew, who provided their families with a comfortable living. Both sons were described as friendly, obedient and respectful, not prone to arguments or fighting. Both went through the French school system, were taught in French, and attended college in Phnom Penh. Until each was approximately twenty years old, the lives of the two were, in most ways, indistinguishable.

Though the two Cambodian sons never met, their paths violently crossed on April 17, 1975, when both experienced Cambodia's political storms at their most violent stages. The older of the two, who by then had assumed the name of Pol Pot, was the precipitating cause of the disaster that nearly destroyed his country and fellow countrymen. Albert Cheng, the other son, was nearly destroyed by those storms. Yet, in being nearly destroyed, he found a new life and is spending the remainder of his life helping undo the destruction.

I have to assume that many who read Albert's story are unfamiliar with Cambodia and the black chapter of the Khmer Rouge. It is virtually impossible to separate Albert's story from the story of the Khmer Rouge, so a brief summary of the geopolitical forces that led to the fall of Cambodia to Pol Pot's forces is included in Section II. And although the name Pol Pot may be familiar to the reader, very few know anything about him or what led him to virtually destroy his own country. An overview of his background and the factors that led a "friendly, obedient boy" down such a destructive path is also included in that section.

The remainder of the book is dedicated to the story of Albert Cheng, his descent into the hell of captivity by the Khmer Rouge, his escape to America, and how he has since found both healing and salvation. The last chapters describe all that he is now doing to help improve the lot of his fellow Cambodians, and to bring to them the message of his newfound Lord and Savior.

And what are we to learn from this story of Albert Cheng, one who has experienced both the worst evil imaginable and the most divine love unimaginable? I asked myself that question at times, as I listened to Albert tell his story and during my attempts to put it into print. Clichés abound, but "It's always darkest before the dawn" feels pathetically trite in the context of the evil of the Killing Fields.

One lesson could be "Never lose hope." That is a good basis for life, but easier said than lived. How do you not lose hope when there are no discernible reasons in your life for having hope? There were times when Albert begged to be killed. And many around him were killed, or died of starvation and untreated illnesses. For them, hope seemed a cruel hoax.

I think for me, and certainly I believe it is what Albert most deeply feels, the lesson to be taken away is the power of the word "grace." From Dictionary.com, one theological definition of grace is "the freely given, unmerited favor and love of God." Perhaps that is the most appropriate definition of the word. You can't be around Albert Cheng very long without being aware of the love of God. But the definition that I think is more relevant is "the influence or spirit of God operating in humans to regenerate or strengthen them."

And that spirit has been made manifest in Albert Cheng. In spite of all that the Khmer Rouge did to him, mentally, emotionally and physically, they were unable to destroy anything in him that the love of God—Grace—could not regenerate and restore.

Sometimes hope does seem futile. Sometimes it feels that life is only darkness, and there will be no dawn. We feel weak, defeated, unable to carry on. I believe Albert Cheng's message to anyone who is at that point in their life is twofold: first, no matter what, there is indeed cause for hope because God loves you. No matter your life's circumstance at the moment, God never abandons you. And second, no matter what your life may entail, God's grace will lead you home.

Del Hayes

Section I
Meet Albert Cheng

Chapter 1

It Was a Peaceful, Joyful Time

He covers the heavens with clouds, he prepares rain for the earth,
he makes grass grow upon the hills.

Psalm 147:8

Cheng Sophanarith, the son who would in later years become known as Albert, sat glued to the floor and fuselage of the tired, dilapidated aircraft like a burr stuck to the tail of a water buffalo. Nervous, but fascinated, he watched the earth rotate below him as the plane banked away from the dusty airstrip it had just departed. Finally, he could begin to breathe again. Fresh air, cooling and less humid as the plane gained altitude, blew across his sweaty face from the large hole in the window next to where he had attached himself when he climbed on board.

Heavy with the familiar scents of rice paddies and the jungle below, the clean air began to calm his pounding heart and clear away the stench of blood from the cargo of beef carcasses that had just been off-loaded from the plane. He did his best to ignore the blood splatters that covered much of the floor and sides of the plane. As his nerves calmed, he peered through the hole, the only portion of the window clean enough to easily see through, and watched the life of his childhood fall away below him.

As the day had approached, the day when he was to leave his family, leave everything and everybody he had known for the seventeen years of his life and start college in far-away Phnom Penh, he had grown increasingly nervous and apprehensive. He had been to his country's capital many times. But always he had traveled on the train, and always with his brothers and sisters along. Never had he lived away from his parents and the security and comfort of his home. Never had he flown in an airplane, never had seen inside one, and he had no idea what to expect of such an experience. What would it feel like to suddenly be snatched away from the earth he loved, floating high in the sky like the birds he so enjoyed watching? What would it be like to be on his own in the big city?

He would have greatly preferred riding the train, but that was out of the question. The railroad had become far too dangerous. Bands of fighters that people were calling "Khmer Rouge" were attacking the trains, and people had already been killed. The national highway had been cut, mined in many places. Flying was the only safe choice.

But his small home town of Pursat had no airport, no airline service. There was a rough dirt strip nearby that the government was using to move supplies and military resources into the area. Somehow, his father had used his connections to get permission for his son to hitch a ride on one of the cargo planes on its return to the capital city.

Saying goodbye to his father, and brothers and sisters, had been even harder than he feared but the time had come and his mother escorted him to the dirt strip. Although he had never been close to an airplane before, even to someone as inexperienced as he the plane that awaited him did not inspire confidence. Its dirty fuselage was patched here and there, causing Albert to wonder for a moment if the patches were covering bullet holes. There were no seats, no seat belts. It was a cargo plane.

He hugged his mother, they shed a few tears, and he climbed aboard, joining the several other men who had already boarded. They were all Caucasian, dressed in blue and white uniforms. Albert had no idea who they were. They chatted amongst themselves, ignoring the young boy stuck at the rear of the plane. Hot, tired and bored, the pilot and co-pilot took their seats up front, anxious to get in the air again.

His throat began to clutch, and he had to stifle gagging from the stench of the hot, stagnant air inside the plane. Grabbing whatever hand-holds as he could find, and wedging his feet against the fuselage, he prepared himself for the take-off as the crew started the engines. Their two large propellers stirred up dust that swirled around the aircraft and seeped into the cargo area through its many cracks and holes.

To his surprise, the take-off, though somewhat bone-rattling as the plane jounced along the bumpy dirt strip, was exhilarating. Now, as he was calming down, his interest began to be drawn to the world below him. From the vantage point of the birds he always envied, he now saw his childhood years sliding along below. It felt strange to be able to see his life spread out below him. *Perhaps that is how the Buddha sees us,* he thought.

Off to the east, through the grime of the window on the opposite side, he recognized the massive Tonle Sap glistening in the sunlight. The waters of that lake, waxing and waning with the monsoon and dry seasons, had been a vital part of the cycle of life of his village, but Albert had never seen it except as flood waters, or from its shore. Its vastness now staggered him, as he could see neither the northern nor southern ends of the lake.

Mother Earth continued to rotate below him, gradually falling farther away, as the plane climbed to altitude and worked its way around to head southeastward to the capital. Pursat, the small town the Cheng family had called home for most of his growing-up years, quickly passed into and out of view through the hole, to be replaced with the greens and browns of the jungle and hills to the west of the town. Through the opposite window he could now begin to make out the river meandering southward from the Tonle Sap to join the mighty Mekong. He wondered if perhaps they might fly over the place of his birth.

Far to the west, he could see the distant mountains that stood between the plains of his home and the Gulf of Thailand. It took a moment, but Albert suddenly realized that in the few minutes since the plane had bounced down the dirt runway to start the flight, he had been transported to the jungles where he had spent so much of his youth. He was astounded. The jungle always seemed so remote. His favorite uncle frequently took Albert with him on his treks into the jungles, but those trips often required two days in the uncle's ox-drawn cart. Detaching himself from the airframe he had been gripping so tightly, he got closer to the hole that was his window to better see the locale of some of the happiest times of his life.

He watched, mesmerized, as the jungle slid along below. Far too fascinated to be aware of time, he noticed that the terrain was changing and a city—much larger than his town of Pursat—that straddled the Tonle Sab River was coming into view. There was little about the city he could recognize from his vantage point of the gods, but he knew it had to be Kampong Chhnang, the city of his birth.

As the city passed out of sight behind him, he knew his virgin flight was soon to end, and his new life of adulthood about to begin. He slumped back against the bulkhead, staring out the hole at the land below. His mind wandered, a jumbled mess of thoughts past, present and future. Thoughts of the future seemed vague, uncertain. What would he do with his life? What did his future hold? No mental image formed, other than images of trying to learn to cope with life in the big city, away from his beloved home and family.

What he could not know, of course, what few in his country perceived, was how drastically and tragically his future and the future of his country was to differ from anything anyone could imagine. For in the countryside passing below his plane were growing forces of evil that would plunge him and his country into a darkness that would nearly consume them all.

Thoughts of present and future were crowded aside by the sight of the countryside below, now growing obviously closer as the plane descended for landing. He closed his eyes, smiling to himself as he thought of his past, his childhood, of pleasant days growing up with his brothers and sisters, of days and nights spent with his uncle in the jungle. There he dwelt, until the hard jolt of an impatient landing brought him back to the present. His future was about to begin.

When we are first coming to know a person we often want to know something of that person's childhood, what their life was like while they were growing up. Part of this comes from natural curiosity, or perhaps simple politeness. But our growing-up years are referred to as the formative years for a reason. Knowing a person's childhood experiences often gives us insight into their personality. This is especially true when that person grew up in an environment so unlike our own, so foreign to anything we might have experienced.

There were stereotypes of what life in Cambodia might have been like, the pictures that came out of the Korean War and Vietnam, and in old encyclopedias: wrinkle-faced old men driving tired oxen with crude wooden yokes pulling tall, wooden-wheeled carts, pictures of women squatting beside open fires, cooking who knew what, with half-naked waifs running nearby, pictures of indistinguishable people hunched over, calf-deep in water, planting rice in small paddies.

We are familiar with such stereotypes of life in those faraway lands, but what we really want to know is whether those stereotypes have any basis in fact. What was life really like growing up in a world so strange, so inscrutable, so unlike anything we had personally experienced? And where better a place to start the story of Albert Cheng than at the very beginning, the place of his birth?

Approximately one third of the way northwestward along National Highway 5 from Phnom Penh to Cambodia's second largest city of Battambang, lies the town of Kampong Chhnang. The town is somewhat of a transportation hub, sitting, as it does, astride both a major highway and the national railroad that also connects Cambodia's two largest cities. To add to that, the town is an important river port on the Tonle Sab River which flows southward from near Thailand, down through the Tonle Sap, to join the Mekong River near Phnom Penh.

Stretching virtually the entire distance from Kampong Chhnang to Battambang, a distance of nearly one hundred miles, is Tonle Sap—loosely translated from Cambodian as "Great Lake."

Tonle Sap is, in a word, a weird lake. During the dry season, it is more like a ten-mile by one-hundred-mile wading pool—barely three feet deep in many places. But all that changes during the monsoon season, when something quite strange happens.

The Mekong River, Cambodia's largest, becomes so swollen that it can no longer handle the flow from the Tonle Sab and water begins to push backward up into Tonle Sap—the river reverses course, and begins to fill the lake—which then, indeed, becomes a great lake. It swells to as much as four times its normal size, and approaches the size of Lake Ontario. Of course, the Tonle Sab river becomes vastly larger, as well. Thus it is that you will see many of the houses and buildings of Kampong Chhnang sitting on stilts, a good ten feet or more off the ground. During the monsoon months, much of the town appears to be floating on the river.

It was in this annually water-logged town of Kampong Chhnang, in 1955, that Albert appeared on the scene. He remembers little of the town, for the simple reason that when he was only two or three years old his parents moved to the much larger city of Battambang. But the Tonle Sap lake, and its annual flooding, influenced life in central Cambodia in countless ways and all of Albert's two decades in his country of birth were lived in near proximity to that iconic lake.

Based on the familiar stereotypes, it would be easy for those of us born and raised in America to imagine Albert telling of being born in one of those thatched huts standing on stilts close to Tonle Sap, of helping his father plant rice in paddies, "fields" that we would have called ponds, of eating nothing but rice while we were having fried chicken, mashed potatoes and gravy. Instead of singing "The Old Rugged Cross," we could picture him burning incense in a temple, listening to monotonic chants of monks.

For much of Cambodia, and for many Cambodians, those stereotypes are quite representative. But Albert did not experience a stereotypical Cambodian life. First and foremost, Albert's father was not the typical rice farmer, slogging along knee-deep in a rice paddy behind a sleepy-looking water buffalo.

"No, Father wasn't a rice farmer. He was an administrator for the railroad from Phnom Penh to Thailand. He was pretty high up, at the time," Albert explained.

France began to get interested in Cambodia in the mid-1800s, for a variety of commercial, political and religious reasons. In the 1860s, when their country eventually became a French Protectorate, life was not without its problems for Cambodians. The French nearly "protected" them right out of their country. They left no doubt as to who was in charge, and who was not.

In spite of that, the French did greatly improve the country. Modern schools were built, offering education never before available in the country. Much of the schooling of Cambodian children was in French, using French methods. Modern Cambodian architecture reflects the French heritage.

A puzzling contradiction to all that, however, is that the French totally neglected advanced education. At the time Albert was born, barely one hundred Cambodian students left the secondary schools each year sufficiently well-prepared to enter technical fields such as medicine and engineering. Most such positions were filled with Vietnamese, because so few Cambodians were qualified—increasing the centuries-old resentment already held toward their neighbor to the east.

Perhaps the most important contribution of all that the French did for the country, though, was the building of roads and railroads. During the first three decades of the twentieth century, over three thousand miles of hard surfaced roads were constructed in the country. And from the late 20s to early 30s, a three-hundred-mile stretch of railroad was constructed from Phnom Penh to Battambang, and later on northward to Poipat, near the border with Thailand. With these improvements in transportation vast new marketing opportunities were opened, both to Cambodian farmers and to the import/export trade with other nations.

But railroads don't run themselves. They need managers, as well as engineers to operate the trains. And at some point in his young married years, or perhaps before he was married—Albert doesn't remember exactly when, for sure—his father, Mr. Cheng, was hired to become a station manager, working for the national railroad. He was trained by French officers, in a French school.

The railroad was an essential transportation link in the country, and obviously very important to the government and to the people of the country. As a manager for the railroad, Albert's father was considered a very important person to those who knew him.

"Father had great respect in the village. Everybody respected Father, and liked him so much. He got along with everybody. I remember he liked music so much. He could not play the instruments, but liked the music. Sometimes at the end of the day, twelve or fifteen villagers with instruments would come to the station and play music. They would stand in a circle and play songs. It was very enjoyable," Albert recalled.

Just as the rice-farmer stereotype did not fit Albert's father, neither did the stereotype of a one-room, thatched-roof hut built on tall stilts to accommodate the monsoon flooding fit their home.

"No, it was brick," Albert said.

Virtually all homes built anywhere close to a river in Cambodia have to be built on ten-foot to twenty-foot stilts to avoid the monsoon floods, and so was Albert's. But where many of the homes were crude thatch huts, Albert's childhood home was far more substantial. Pictures of the house in which they lived show a modern style house that appears to be of brick and stucco design, on tall, brick columns. At the time the picture was taken, after the fall of the Khmer Rouge, the house had been taken over by the Cambodian military for offices.

The government provided not only modern, well-constructed housing for its railroad managers, but also sufficient income for a secure, upper middle-class lifestyle for the Cheng family. For good or ill, the job also required the family to move periodically. Not only did Albert have to move from his birth place of Kampong Chhnang to Battambang when he was about two years old, the family had to spend a brief period living in Poipat, near the Thai border, then move again to Battambang.

Albert has few memories of living in Cambodia's second largest city. The Cheng family again had to move when he was about six years old, leaving Battambang to move to the town of Pursat midway between Battambang and Phnom Penh, west of Tonle Sap lake. Albert's formative years began while the family lived in Pursat, and most of his childhood memories come from that time.

Pursat was then, and still is, an "off the beaten track" sort of town. The website www.tourismcambodia.com has little to say about the town, but touts the countryside in which it is located:

> The provincial capital of Pursat is also called Pursat town. The city is located right in the middle between the Tonle Sap and the Cardamom Mountains on the riverbanks of the Stung Pursat. There isn't that much to do in that small town, so most of the tourists coming here are on their way to Battambang or Phnom Penh.

> Most of the country...is the Krâvanh Mountains, or literally called "Cardamom Mountains". This is a green, forested mountain range in the southwestern part of the province,

near to the border with Thailand. The highest elevation is the 1,813m (5,892 feet) high Phnom Aural in the Southeast corner of the country. Pursat offers a relatively easy way to enter this fantastic ecological wonder.

Pursat, it seems, was the proverbial "old shoe" fit for Albert's personality.

"It was very peaceful, a very joyful life," he said, smiling, remembering his life growing up in Pursat.

"I remember being together as a family, with Mother and Father, and my brothers and sisters. As a young boy, I was dressed in a school uniform of blue khaki pants and white shirt. We had a maid who lived with us. She usually laid my clothes out and got me dressed. We attended school most of the day, then played games around the train station and nearby village after school. Most of the time, we played badminton on a court in the railroad station compound. Sometimes we played kickball, or a lawn game with balls. I don't know what you call it. It was sort of like your croquet."

Like the children of most families, the Cheng children were responsible for assisting in household duties. But unlike the stereotype of American children, at least as portrayed on contemporary television, they welcomed the opportunity to do things for their parents.

"Cambodians have great respect for our fathers and mothers. My brothers and sisters and I just loved doing things for our parents. It was an honor. Not in the sense of because we had to. It was such an honor to do things for them. We would fight to see who got to do something for Father and Mother, because we respected them so much."

Rice was a daily staple in Cambodian diets, but Albert said they also ate quite a lot of fish and chicken. Sometimes they had beef or pork from the local market. But with no refrigeration, meat had to be consumed while fresh.

"Nobody had a refrigerator," Albert said. "We had electricity; just a light on a wire from the ceiling. But nobody had a refrigerator. When you got a chicken, or other meat, you had to just eat it right away."

There was more to the diet than just rice and staples. There were other delicacies.

"I had one uncle who was a rice farmer, but also a mountain man. I liked to help work in his rice fields. This uncle, during the wet season, the monsoons, would go out in rice paddies and catch frogs. There were just thousands and thousands of frogs in the paddies. We would fry legs, or make sweet and sour frog legs. They were so good. We also liked stuffed frogs," Albert added.

The railroad, and the trains, played a big role in Albert's childhood memories, especially the old steam engines. He told of often going to the station where his father worked, to watch the trains come and go, and watch as his father, the manager, got freight on and off the cars.

"The trains were still steam engines, when I was young," Albert said, "and I so enjoyed seeing them and hearing the whistle. But they converted to diesel later on, from the French. Engineers would blow the whistle at farmers in rice fields, sometimes. They had lots of accidents due to water buffalo and cattle wandering across the tracks, I remember Father telling me."

Having a father who worked for the railroad had its fringe benefits, beyond a comfortable living. The children got to ride on the train quite regularly, as guests of the railroad. It gave Albert and his brothers and sisters, an opportunity to see his country, and its capital city, in ways not available to most children of the country.

"Oh, I enjoyed it so much, it was such a joy inside of me," Albert said. "Because Father worked for the railroad, all us brothers and sisters got to go to the capital of Phnom Penh every other Friday or Saturday. They gave us this railroad ID. When they saw the ID, they let us pass because we were part of the train family. It was such a privilege for us. We traveled night and day. I remember we had such good times. Different stations along the way had various kinds of Cambodian foods.

"We would get off at the stations where we knew they had food we liked. We liked to stop at Mongn station, for example. I loved this place because they knew how to make the 'sparrow fries.' During the season, the whole sky was just black with these little birds, and they would catch them in traps and make the fries. They would serve them along with hot rice wrapped in banana leaves, or lotus leaves, with fresh coconut juice for drinking. They also served frog fries, and stuffed frogs, as well as smoked fish in bamboo sticks. We always enjoyed eating there." Albert didn't elaborate on how "sparrow fries" were made. Perhaps that's just as well.

Like the children of families around the world, most of Albert's growing-up years were dedicated to attending school. Cambodian schools, for those villages large enough to have a school, were modeled after the French school system.

"It was opposite of in America. We start at the twelfth level, and work up to first level. At about the fifth level, then we take the exam to see if we can continue on with our education. If we pass, we go on to advanced school, called lycée," he explained.

Whereas in American schools a student is advanced each year from grade to grade, assuming they meet the appropriate standards, the French system relied on two major exams for advancement to each higher level of schooling. The first exam was to permit the student to leave primary schooling and enter what might be considered high school.

"I took it around age fourteen or fifteen. It was a big, big exam," he emphasized, waving his arms in the air. "I remember children who did not live in the village where the exam was given had to come live there for the whole week, while they took the exam. Many did not pass it."

The scope and scale, and ultimate importance, of that end-of-year exam can hardly be overemphasized. If passed, the student received the certificate for leaving primary school, the *Certificat d'Etudes Primaires Complémentaires*. Without it, further schooling was essentially unavailable.

"If passed, then you go on to the equivalent of high school, taught locally if your village is big enough to have the school. I studied math, science, chemistry, geography, taught in French and Khmer (the native language of Cambodia). At the end of high school, around age seventeen or eighteen, I had to pass another big exam to qualify to move on to college (in Phnom Penh)."

Albert spoke little of his accomplishments in school but it would be easy to infer that he did well, based on the fact that he had to deal with learning French as well as learning his subjects—and that he managed to pass the comprehensive exams that so many failed. Based on those accomplishments, one would have to assume he would have been equally successful in a chosen career. Albert never got the chance to have a career of his choice, but the question did arise as to whether he had some idea of what he would have wanted to do, had he been able to graduate from college.

"No, not really. I didn't really have any idea, while I was going to school," Albert said of his thoughts about his future. "My brothers, they had all sorts of ideas. The older one wanted to be in the medical field. He had just one more year, then he could go to study medicine in France, but the Khmer Rouge destroyed all that. They killed him. No, I never thought much about a career. I mostly enjoyed my home and family, and being out in the woods."

Although Albert's childhood was perhaps more "middle class" than that of many children of the time and locale, in many respects there was little about his childhood that was significantly different from others in his village. He was likable, obedient, and enjoyed playing games. He loved and respected his parents, as well as his brothers and sisters. Seen in retrospect, the combination of having the advantages of a middle-class life with privileges such as the frequent trips to Phnom Penh, while at the same time being exposed to the harsher realities of rice farming and the ways of the jungle, gave Albert a balance that few enjoyed. Thus, he was not only able to survive the desperate years of harsh labor and treatment under the Khmer Rouge, but was also better prepared to adapt to the complexities of modern urban life in America.

Albert admits to being a "city boy" while he was growing up, but it was being out in the woods, the jungles near his home, with his uncle that had the greatest influence on him during those formative years. If there were any one constant then, it was his longing to better understand what was beyond the physical world around him.

Those days in the jungle, where he would often spend hours meditating, influenced his early thoughts about his spiritual life. It was deep in the jungle where the seeking and longing for something felt, but unknown, became so much a part of him, that stayed with him and haunted him for many of his years. But it was also those days and nights spent in the jungle that prepared him for later experiences, and literally saved his life as years later he attempted to escape to Thailand.

Chapter 2

Where Is God?

I lift up my eyes to the hills. From where will my help come?
Psalm 121:1 (NRSV)

"We had been pushing our way through the jungle since early sunrise," the old man related. "Now the sun was high above us. I had grown very tired, and sweat covered my face and body. I decided to sit down at the base of a large tree to rest. I guess sleep overcame me. I felt I was having a dream. Suddenly I felt cool, like my body was wrapped in something cool. I struggled awake, and opened my eyes. I was in shock! I was completely wrapped in the coils of a great python. It was getting ready to crush me, to have me for its meal."

"What did you do? How did you survive?" asked his horrified listener, eyes wide with disbelief. It was well understood that once in the grip of a python, nothing could escape its crushing force. The outcome was always known, always inevitable. Yet, here was one telling of surviving such a thing. How could that be?

"It is not well known. But when a python is ready to crush an animal, it pushes its tail up into the nostril, to penetrate the brain.

When the tail of the python began pushing against my face, I bit its tail off," he said, laughing aloud at the memory of it. "The python unwrapped me and hurried off into the jungle."

"My Uncle Hank liked to tell that story about a friend of his," Albert said, laughing as he related the story. "I always enjoyed hearing it."

That was one of many stories Albert told of his years growing up as a sometimes-jungle-boy. One facet of Albert's personality was frequently evident: he loved the outdoors, to be in the jungle, at one with nature. His lifelong quest for spiritual answers, his "seeking" for that which he missed but could not define, began in quiet meditation deep in the jungle. Getting to go on those jungle trips was a fortuitous result of his family tree.

On one branch of that tree was a favorite uncle, on his mother's side, who was a rice farmer but also a mountain man. Some of Albert's fondest memories from childhood were when Uncle Hangh—or Uncle "Hank," as Albert called him—took him into the jungle to hunt and commune with nature. They spent a lot of time there, and Albert learned the ways of the jungle—learned to hunt, to find his way, and to survive. How much that early training contributed to his surviving the trek through the jungles to Thailand to escape the Khmer Rouge can only be speculated, but it must have been considerable.

Albert was young, and doesn't remember exactly where Uncle Hank took him, but it could well have been the Cardamom Mountains, in Pursat Province. This green, forested mountain range, with some peaks in excess of 5,000 feet above sea level, is an ecological wonder and now a tourist attraction. Albert lived in Pursat at the time, and his uncle farmed not too far from Pursat. It seems reasonable to believe it was in this natural wonder that

Albert experienced his "Jungle Book" times that were so obviously important to him.

"Uncle Hank, my mother's brother, was a rice farmer who lived on the outskirts of Pursat, by the river," Albert explained. "He would take his water buffalo and cart, and take me into the woods. It would take sometimes two days to get there. We would spend a lot of time in the woods. Trees were huge, very tall. I learned to climb them like a monkey. I just put my toes in the bark and climbed up. The overhead growth was sometimes so dense that not even the sunlight could penetrate. It would be dark all day. And there was lots of undergrowth, but there were sometimes paths to walk in. You had to follow the paths to get through.

"In the jungle, or woods, the earth was very rich with decayed compost. If I ate a watermelon, and spit out the seeds, two weeks later you could see the watermelon starting to grow from the seeds."

Another part of his experiences with his Uncle Hank, and one of the more enjoyable elements of his childhood, was hunting in the jungle.

"Uncle Hank had ten dogs, trained for different types of game—dogs for deer, for birds, and so forth," Albert said. "He used them to catch game, which he cooked for meals. I liked to listen to the dogs when they hunted game."

Most of the Cambodian jungle, as Albert described it, was "very heavy, with dense undergrowth. The sun couldn't penetrate some of it." Even for someone experienced at being in the jungle it was still possible to get lost, as Albert confessed he did on some occasions. And how does one who is lost in the jungle get rescued?

"I would climb a tall tree and yell real loud," he explained, laughing at himself. "The dogs would hear me and come find me. Uncle Hank would hear them barking, and find me."

"I loved being in the jungle with Uncle Hank. It was like…" he had to pause, searching for the word, "spiritual, for me. I could sit out there and just meditate for hours, and be at peace. And sometimes, I would climb to the tip top of the tallest tree on a hill, just to feel like I was closest to whatever spirit was up there, out there. I wanted to be close to it."

To the Western mind, Albert's beloved jungle would not be a place of peaceful meditation, or serenity. Jungles are typically portrayed as being rather dangerous, with tigers and poisonous snakes, and all that unpleasantness. We Americans would be thinking far more of being eaten by a tiger, than of meditating and finding peace.

"Oh, yes, there were tigers in the jungles. By the way, do you know how to confront the tiger? You must stare them down," he said, answering his own question. "Look them straight in the eye. Don't blink. In a little while, they turn and go away.

"Sometimes, Uncle Hank told me, the people would carry an umbrella in the jungle, to scare the tiger," he added. "If they see a tiger, when it is close, they pop open the umbrella. It is so big, and such a surprise, the tiger runs off."

Well, perhaps.

But there was far more to Albert's trips to the jungle than simply enjoying hunting and listening to jungle-lore stories with Uncle Hank. There was an aspect of his jungle experiences that raised more questions than answers. According to Albert, there was more going on out in his jungle than what we normally associate with jungle life.

"Uncle Hank encountered what he called the 'magical' people in the jungle," Albert related. "These people are very truthful—if they say it, they have to do it. It is their nature, they don't know how to lie. They spend all their time in the woods. They can just appear, and disappear.

"Uncle Hank told me one time he was out in the jungle, and didn't have any cookware to fix his meal. He said he just kneeled down and prayed, and these people came to him, like in a dream, and told him where to go. Then in the morning, he said he just walked to the spot where he was shown in his dream. He dug into the ground, and sure enough, there was a pot and plates and things to cook with.

"That was when I began to realize that there is something that goes on, something in the spirit, that I didn't understand," he admitted.

And did he personally ever encounter those people while in the woods?

"Umm...I...I didn't. I didn't," he answered, after a long hesitation. "And that was the thing I longed for."

An obvious question was whether these "magical" people were real, or whether his uncle imagined them, in some way. But Albert was quite emphatic.

"No, it had nothing to do with the imagination. These are real people. The person who ran into these people is my brother, Sarindy. Somehow he, too, got into the spiritual aspect. He came to the States (after the fall of the Khmer Rouge), to Houston. Somehow he got a calling, and left his wife and family to go back to the jungle. He was gone for three years. There is so much going on in the spiritual world, out there in the jungle, beyond our understanding."

All that sort of thing admittedly generates little understanding and raises lots of incredulity, if not downright skepticism, for the Western mind. One of the most obvious aspects of Cambodian culture, one which has permeated it from top to bottom since two or three centuries before the birth of Christ, is the near-universal adherence to Theravada Buddhism. As discussed in some detail in later chapters, its influence on the country, its politics, and the behavior of its people is ubiquitous and can't be overemphasized.

Lift the cover of Buddhism, however, and look underneath at the routine day-to-day beliefs of the people, and two lesser known aspects of Cambodian culture also become apparent. Although not so obvious as Buddhism, these two facets of the culture have had equal, perhaps even greater, influence on the Cambodian people for centuries, even to modern times.

First, Animism, or spirit worship, has been part of the life of indigenous people of Indochina and Indonesia for untold centuries, long before the arrival of Buddhism. Animism is the belief that inanimate objects—trees, rocks, rivers, mountains—have spirits that can affect the well-being of adherents. It involves ancestor worship as well as spirit worship, and permeates Cambodian life at all levels. Animism is as much a part of daily life for many Cambodians as is Buddhism. Animist populations are known to exist in the mountains of northeast Cambodia, and one could easily assume that the "magical people" experienced by Albert's Uncle Hank were of this sort.

The other facet of Cambodian culture that soon becomes apparent is that superstition and the occult have also been an integral part of life for untold generations. The use of charms, fetishes, belief in the magic of the krama—the checkered, colorful symbolic scarf often seen being worn around the neck—as well as various rituals and libations are all an essential part of life. Although the practice may be diminishing in modern times, and Christianity is making inroads, these aspects were very much a part of life as Albert grew up.

It was apparent that the jungle life deeply influenced Albert's personality, for it was in the jungle where he first developed a sense of spirituality, an awareness that life held more than met the eye and whetted his thirst for some form of spiritual peace. That early development never left him, and it is out in nature that he still feels most at home. In spite of all else that happened to him, it has been his spiritual journey, seeking that undefined "something" that would give him the inner peace that he cherished, that has had the most impact on him throughout his life.

Another obvious element in his spiritual life and his seeking for peace was his upbringing and his early training in Buddhism, which permeates every aspect of Cambodian daily life and in many respects is as much a part of the life of the average villager as breathing. Certainly, being raised in that environment influenced Albert.

Cambodia lies across a form of cultural fault line, separating the mystical beliefs of Buddhism and Brahmanism of India from the more logical, practical teachings of Confucianism of China, Vietnam and countries to the east. That divide, those cultural conflicts, played a significant role not only in the geo-politics of the area but also in Albert's experiences after coming to America, where the spiritualism of the East met the pragmatism of the West.

Of course, not every Cambodian is a strongly orthodox Buddhist. As in all religions, some are strong believers while others merely pay lip service. And it is also true, as it is in many religions, that the young are often not as devout as their elders. It appears that Albert was somewhat in the middle of that spectrum.

"Mother and Father were Buddhist, of course," he said. "But I saw myself more as a 'seeker.' I just loved to spend a lot of time deep in the woods, in the jungle, in a sort of meditative state. It was heaven on earth for me. That is why I liked so much for my

Uncle Hank to take me into the woods with him. I was seeking for something, what would be the word…something beautiful out of nature. I didn't know what it was, but just something that would draw me into it. It was like heaven on earth to me. I couldn't understand it, at that young age. I was just at peace in the woods."

We are, especially in our childhood, a product of both our environment—our families and neighbors—and our training. Many of the older generations of Albert's family were very devout Buddhists. Albert's grandmother, for example, paid to have a local temple built so people of the village could worship without having to go to another village. When he was approximately fourteen, Albert received training and guidance in Buddhist rituals and chants from a monk in a local temple. He respected the "faith of his fathers" and was influenced by it. Meditation became an important part of his personality.

Even at a young age, however, Albert often sensed that there was something to life that he was missing, something that he wanted to be a part of his life but that he could neither define nor find. Although trained in its ways, Buddhism didn't satisfy those internal longings.

"I kept asking, 'Is there a God? Where is God?'" Albert said, at one point. "I felt I was always seeking, but never could find the answer."

Those questions were to get answered for him, in dramatic fashion, later in life. But during his early years there were only questions, only seeking. Perhaps it was the ambivalence on the subject of God that resulted in his Buddhist faith failing to answer his questions. Buddha was human, and is not considered to be God by Buddhists. The faith is neither predicated on the existence of a monotheistic god, nor does it reject the existence of one or more gods.

According to the Buddha, man has the capacity to develop within himself a pure mind and perfect love—god is not essential to human development and perfection. But until a person achieves that perfection, there is only an endless cycle of birth, aging, and death as the individual attempts to adhere to the Four Noble Truths and finally find release. By and large, all that was beyond the grasp of most Cambodians. The best they could do each day was to try to build up good "merit" and try to avoid building up bad "merit"—and hope for the best.

That longing, the seeking, would consume Albert for many years of his life, and not find resolution until long after what he called his years of "darkness" under the Khmer Rouge. He was to find his peace not in the jungles of his home, or the faith of his childhood, but in a Christian church in a place called Texas, on the far side of the globe.

Section II
The Big Picture

Chapter 3

Peeling the Onion

Help, Lord; for there is no longer any that is godly; for the faithful have vanished from among the sons of men. Every one utters lies to his neighbor; with flattering lips and a double heart they speak.

Psalm 12:1-2

Any attempt to present a brief history of Cambodia and the tragedy of the Khmer Rouge soon becomes an exercise best described by the quote sometimes attributed to Mark Twain: "I didn't have time to write a short book, so I wrote a long one." Nevertheless, what follows is an attempt to present a brief history of the events that led to the ascendancy of the Khmer Rouge.

"Why does it matter?" you might ask. "How does something that happened decades ago affect the story of Albert Cheng?"

That would appear to be a relevant question. The answer is this: It is virtually impossible to read of Albert's experiences at the hands of the Khmer Rouge, read of all that happened to him and the millions like him, and not ask yourself, "How did such a thing happen?"

The experiences of Albert Cheng cannot be rightfully told without peeling at least a few layers off the onion that is that history, with all its convoluted twists and turns, its often-corrupt and Machiavellian politicians and leaders, and the geo-political tug-of-war contending in Southeast Asia between democratic and communist powers.

Peel very many layers off that onion, and what will be exposed is the "lost glory of Angkor." From about the ninth through the thirteenth centuries A.D., the Khmer civilization dominated what is now Southeast Asia in much the way that Alexander the Great had dominated the Middle East, centuries earlier. What is now Cambodia, much of Thailand, Laos and Vietnam were all ruled by a series of Cambodian kings from an elaborate capital city and temple complex called Angkor Wat, which is today's number-one tourist attraction in Cambodia. But the tide eventually turned, as usually happens, and the golden empire of the Khmer faded, never to return. That lost glory resulted in a form of national inferiority complex that affects Cambodia, and Cambodians, to this very day.

For the next several centuries, Cambodia entered what some historians call its Dark Ages. Its empire steadily dwindled as one battle for territory after another was lost. Siam—now Thailand— steadily laid claim to land to the north. Vietnam, using a program of establishing settlements along the Mekong Delta then laying claim to the settled land, took possession of what later became South Vietnam. To avoid further losses to Vietnam, what remained of the Khmer empire became a protectorate of Siam.

The people merely existed during those degrading losses, surviving the way they always had: by matching their lives to the dry and monsoon seasons, raising rice and catching fish. That began to change in the 1800s, when empire-building on the part of the powers of Europe came into bloom. India came under the control of England, and France began to take an interest in the resources of Southeast Asia.

For many years in the 1800s, Cambodia had been ruled by Siam and Vietnam. King Norodom of Cambodia, ever fearful of his ancient foes to either side of him, looked to the French for protection. In 1863 he signed an agreement for Cambodia to become a French Protectorate. By the late 1860s, France had gained control of Vietnam and Laos as well, forming what became known as French Indochina. Cambodia began what was to become nearly a century of French domination and influence that continued, with some disruptions, until years after World War II ended.

King Norodom died in 1904, to be succeeded by Preah Bat Sisowath, who died in 1927 and was succeeded by his son, Prince Sisowath Monivong. During the reign of Monivong, things began to heat up as the world moved inexorably toward world war. In 1930, Ho Chi Minh formed the ICP—the Indochina Communist Party—in Vietnam, with the express goal of overthrowing the French and ejecting them from the region.

It later become clear that Ho Chi Minh was not being magnanimous toward his neighbors, hoping to free all of Southeast Asia from foreign control. His intention, his plan, was to defeat the French and bring the region under the control of his party. Few Cambodians were aware of such intentions, and the idea of overthrowing the French appealed to many of them. As a consequence, the ICP was favorably received by many Cambodians, before its real purpose became known.

When France fell to the German armies at the beginning of World War II, not only did France come under the control of the puppet Vichy government under Marshall Petain, but in a form of "guilt by association," Cambodia came under the same control. It was not long before Japan invaded Vietnam, and occupied Cambodia. The Japanese, allies of Germany, allowed the Vichy

French to stay in control. Thailand, also an ally of Japan, saw its chance and took control of much of northern Cambodia. It was not long before both countries, Japan and Thailand, began severe oppression of the Cambodians, but Monivong was powerless to do anything about it. He retired in 1941, and died the same year.

His son should have been the king's successor, but the French wanted someone they believed would be more compliant to their interests, so they installed the nineteen-year-old Norodom Sihanouk instead.

As the Allied forces pushed steadily forward across Europe and the South Pacific, pushing the German and Japanese armies ever rearward, Cambodia experienced a jolting change.

Japan had been steadily losing ground to the Allies, and wanted to retain the favor of the Southeast Asian countries. Japanese forces in Cambodia staged what became, in effect, a coup. Without warning, French government officials were arrested and civilians interned. King Sihanouk was prodded to declare that the French were "incapable of providing protection." The unthinkable had happened. French rule collapsed overnight, and Cambodia was declared an independent nation.

Independence didn't last. With the defeat of Japan and Germany, the French moved back in. Sihanouk signed an agreement with the French government providing for the resumption of French rule, but with Cambodian autonomy. Nevertheless, where independence from the French was concerned, for Cambodians the cat was out of the bag. For the moment, perhaps, independence from the French might not be attainable, but for a growing number of Cambodians the idea was not out of mind. And another tectonic shift was taking place on the political scene.

For centuries, governance of Cambodia was accepted as the sole province of the palace. With independence now an ideal and a goal, many Cambodians were no longer willing to accept being excluded from a role in governing their country. Small guerilla groups began to form in the protection of the mountain jungle regions, making occasional forays against the establishment. The young Sihanouk, wanting to appear to be a modernizer, allowed the formation of the first political parties—though he remained very much in control of the government.

Largely unnoticed however, developments occurring in neighboring North Vietnam were to ultimately play a far greater role in the life of Cambodia. Ho Chi Minh and his Indochina Communist Party had taken control of Hanoi. For some time, they attempted to negotiate their way out from under French control as part of the long range goal of bringing all of Indochina under one Communist-controlled "Democratic Republic of Indochina." When negotiating failed to accomplish that objective, Ho Chi Minh turned to armed revolt. In support of that, he arranged an agreement with Thailand to secretly move arms into North Vietnam to support the "revolution."

Northeastern Cambodia provided the only viable route to supply those arms, and to protect this vital logistical route it became essential to bring the area under Communist control. Small cadres of Vietnamese Communists moved into eastern Cambodia to establish bases and control. Nobody bothered to ask the Cambodian villagers if they wanted such control, and one important historical reality was ignored—that was the fact that for essentially all of history, the Cambodians and Vietnamese hated each other to the core. The Vietnamese considered Cambodians to be illiterate and indolent, while Cambodians considered Vietnamese to be arrogant and condescending. Consequently, progress was slow but the ICP cadres persisted and over time began to quietly take control of northeastern Cambodia.

The battle of Ho Chi Minh's forces against the French—the first Vietnam war—began in earnest and the future fate of Cambodia was sealed. But few Cambodians, or leaders of other countries, comprehended at the time the significance of what was quietly taking place in the remote jungles of eastern Cambodia.

Much like contending toddlers, all tugging on their mother's skirt to gain her full attention, the history of Cambodia had been a history of contending forces. And never was that more true than during the years following the end of World War II, through the Vietnam wars and finally to the fall of the central government in 1975.

First of these contending forces, and perhaps the most important, was the intensifying desire on the part of many Cambodians to be free of the French after nearly a century of colonialism. Second was the growing determination to wrest control of the government of their country from the realm of the palace, to force Sihanouk to permit elected officials to share power. And third was the growing menace of the Viet Minh forces of Ho Chi Minh to gain control of Cambodia and bring it into a Communist Indochina. Supporters of each of these factors became increasingly dependent on violence to advance their cause, and in a real sense everybody was fighting everybody else.

Those trying to force Sihanouk to open his government joined forces with guerilla groups calling themselves "Freedom Fighters," who had for some time been staging raids against the French, and hence against the government. Sihanouk and the French in turn attacked these groups. Students staged protests, some of which turned violent, in opposition to the French. Indigenous Communist groups—primarily students (including, as it turned out, the student who came to be known as Pol Pot) who had convinced themselves while attending college in Paris that armed revolution was the only way to get rid of the French—were aligning themselves with the Viet Minh.

Viet Minh soldiers in Cambodia began using scorched-earth tactics to force Cambodian peasants to support them. Incomprehensible violence and brutality were practiced by all factions. Assassination squads were formed, grenades tossed into theaters. It seemed the country was descending into chaos. Finally, the French had enough, and called it quits. On November 9, 1953, a *modus vevendi* was signed and the French government handed military and governmental control of Cambodia over to the Sihanouk government.

In that one act most of the contending forces lost their Cause Célèbre, and had to redefine their enemy. With the French now gone, King Sihanouk had to become the "boogeyman" and was quickly labeled as the lackey of the French. Ergo, it now became necessary to get rid of Sihanouk as the source of evil in the empire.

Hoping to overthrow the Sihanouk government, the Viet Minh planned a major offensive against Sihanouk's forces. On April 12, 1954, just months before Albert's birth, Viet Minh forces mined the railway from Phnom Penh to Battambang, derailing the train. The soldiers then proceeded to brutally torture and kill the passengers, burning many to death. Over one hundred died in the massacre.

One can only wonder how that act of violence against the railroad affected Albert's father. As a high level administrator for the railroad, he must have been apprehensive of the future, if government forces could no longer be trusted to defend the railway. What future did he see for his growing family? Did he fear for his own safety? For his livelihood? Were his fears and apprehensions felt by his family?

"No, I don't remember much of that," Albert said, when asked if he had any memory of his father talking about such raids, or whether he had expressed any concerns about the safety of the railroad. "I do remember, Father had a large revolver. When we were in Battambang, I remember he carried it, sometimes."

But just as it seemed that the country was descending into open warfare, a major event changed the future—at least temporarily. Peace talks were being held in Geneva, Switzerland, to determine the fate of the area, as the French pulled out. After long and contentious negotiations, Sihanouk managed to get the territories back from Thailand that had been usurped during World War II. Vietnam was divided into North and South Vietnam—setting the stage for the second Vietnam war—but Cambodia was left intact, with Sihanouk in control.

In that one event, all the immediate causes for warfare evaporated. The Viet Minh forces, having gained little traction in Cambodia, withdrew to North Vietnam, to fight another day. The local Cambodian Communist groups skulked off into the jungle to figure out how to redefine their enemy and plot a new struggle. The Freedom Fighters, who had been fighting against French control and the Sihanouk government, also temporarily faded into the jungle. Many of them accepted an offer of clemency from the Sihanouk government and laid down their arms. Contention between Sihanouk and those wanting to open his government to elections continued, but without the violence.

What Albert remembers, then, as the "peaceful, joyful" times of his childhood were primarily a matter of good fortune and timing. Up to the time Albert was about twelve or fourteen years old, Cambodia experienced the least open fighting and warfare since World War II. But of course, it wasn't to last. Local, as well as geo-political, forces once again began to pull the country apart. The bloodiest period of Cambodia's history was beginning to take root in its jungles.

Chapter 4

Pol Pot: Prelude to Insanity

On every side the wicked prowl, as vileness is exalted among the sons of men.

Psalm 12:8

Genocide is defined as the deliberate and systematic extermination of a national, racial, political or cultural group. Horrific examples of the practice are well documented, with the Holocaust under Adolph Hitler, millions of Russians dying under Joseph Stalin, and millions of Chinese dying under Mao Tse Tung. In actual numbers, not as many died under Pol Pot and the Khmer Rouge as died in those better-known examples; estimates suggest one-and-a-half million to two million Cambodians died under Pol Pot. Compared to the population of the country, however, it was perhaps even worse, with estimates varying from fifteen to thirty percent of all Cambodians dying during the four years of that horror.

In one respect, the only difference between those various crimes against humanity was one of magnitude—the number of dead under each tyrant. But in one other respect, the extermination of Cambodians by Pol Pot was unique. Hitler, Stalin and Mao Tse

Tung were well-known public figures. What they were doing to the people of their country may not have come to light for some time, but in each case the man was a public figure, the leader of his country and well known. Not so for Pol Pot.

Secrecy was fundamental to the success of Pol Pot and his attempt to gain control of Cambodia. Not until 1976, after the fall of the Lon Nol government, did anyone but his closest staff know who this secretive figure was. Indeed, many wondered if such a person even existed. Pol Pot once was quoted as saying, "They may know who I am, but they don't know what I am." At the time, he was but an obscure political activist known by his given name of Saloth Sar. No one outside his inner circle, not the Lon Nol government, not the U.S. Central Intelligence Agency, not the intelligence agencies of other Western countries, remotely suspected that the shy former student was the power behind the Khmer Rouge.

Who, then, was this mysterious figure? Where did he come from? What caused him to transform into the monstrosity that he became? Just as it is not the purpose of this book to be a history of Cambodia, neither is it a biography of Pol Pot. But in truth this is not just the story of Albert Cheng, but is the tale of two sons of Cambodia—born in close proximity, and raised in similar circumstances. The story of the Khmer Rouge, and of Albert Cheng, cannot be separated from the story of Pol Pot.

Travel the national highway from Phnom Penh northward toward the city of Siem Reap, through the rice country along the east side of the great lake of Tonle Sap, and you will pass through the town of Kampong Thom. It's not an overly large town, with a population of perhaps ten thousand, and has little to distinguish it other than being the provincial capital of the province by the same name. Just before you cross the bridge over the muddy river Sen in the middle of the town, there is a street off to the left.

Follow that street along the east side of the river for a half mile, or a little more, and you will come to a nondescript fishing village on the bank of the river, known as Prek Sbauv. It was, and still is, virtually indistinguishable from hundreds of other villages in Cambodia, consisting of a scraggly collection of thatched huts on stilts. This tiny village would hardly warrant more than a passing glance were it not for the son born there years ago to the Saloth family. His parents named him Sar. Although some official records show that Sar was born in 1928, other records indicate an earlier birth, in 1925.

There was little to set Sar apart from other sons born to other families in the village, with the exception that while Sar was quite young his father had prospered when the price of rice increased greatly. By the time Sar was born, his father owned considerably more rice acreage than most, and was considered by his neighbors to be wealthy. Other than being significantly larger, their home was similar to the others in the village—a single room in which all the family ate and slept.

By all accounts, Sar was an agreeable, docile child described by those who knew him as friendly, adorable and obedient. Reflecting back on their childhood, an eighty-year-old resident of the village—Sar's younger brother, Nhep—remembered his brother as a child "who wouldn't harm a fly" ("We Just Tried To Survive," www.rfa.org). In his book, *Pol Pot*, Philip Short describes Sar's childhood as one of peacefulness and tranquility, a serene time of swimming in the river and playing games with his siblings and other children in the village. As he grew, Sar had the reputation of being one usually seen with a friendly smile on his face. But over the years, that smile became enigmatic, an impervious, inscrutable mask, hiding whatever thoughts and feelings might have been lurking behind the smiling eyes.

That serenity, the tranquil rural life of the fisherman and rice farmer, was illusory. Those early years were not a harbinger for the way in which the life of Saloth Sar was to play out, for the world in which he was to come of age was not a tranquil place. Outside his village of Prek Sbauv, the world was rapidly coming apart at the seams. By the time Sar was in the equivalent of high school, Germany had invaded Poland, the Japanese had bombed Pearl Harbor, and the world was plunged into global war—a war that dramatically affected and altered the politics of his homeland. That war ended, only to reveal the beginning of a power struggle between East and West that continues today.

Sar's older brothers had been sent to the *wat*, or Buddhist temple, in nearby Kampong Thom for schooling. But Sar's father decided that he could afford to send his younger children to formal schooling. The eldest son of the Saloth family had earlier moved to Phnom Penh, so another older brother of Sar's, Chhay, was sent to live with that brother and attend the new Western-style primary grade school built and operated by the French. When Sar turned nine years old, it was his turn and he was also sent off to school at Phnom Penh.

Before attending school, however, (in what would later become a cruel irony in light of the sadistic destruction that was to be wrought by Sar—Pol Pot—on the Buddhist monks and *wats*) Sar first lived a year at a large monastery near the royal palace as an apprentice monk. This may seem unusual, but in fact it was not. Most young men were expected to spend a year, or more, learning the mysteries and disciplines of Theravada Buddhism, then leave to lead a normal secular life.

In a real sense, this year was little different than being required to spend a tour in the military. It was expected, and you just did it. Though Buddhism was part and parcel of life in Cambodia, its precepts seemed above the heads of most of the citizens. The subtleties of achieving perfection, rejection of the self, Nirvana, all such concepts were largely the realm of the monks. To the average citizen, life came down to the old saw of "Do good, get good. Do bad, get bad."

To have a son spend a year in the temple, in the presence of the Buddha and influence of the monks, was in the view of the parents a means of achieving merit. So the sons went, served their tours, and left. During his year in the temple, Sar learned contemplation and meditation. He was subjected to the rigid codes of self-discipline that were fundamental to a Buddhist monk, in which individual thought and initiative were subordinated to unquestioning obedience.

At age ten, Sar left the monastery and entered Ecole Miche, a Catholic school near the government palace in Phnom Penh, to begin his formal schooling. Classes were taught in French by Vietnamese and French Catholic Fathers. Sar was an indifferent student and failed to pass the exam that permitted him to leave primary schooling until age eighteen, having been held back two years in his attempts to pass the exam.

He took the exam to enter the prestigious Lycée Sisowath, but failed it. Later he was able to enter the newly opened college Preah Sihanouk in Kampong Cham, fifty miles north of Phnom Penh on the Mekong River. It was during this time, in the early 1940s, during the war, that major political shifts were beginning to occur in Cambodia. But Sar, at that age, was largely unaware of, and uninterested in, most of it.

Sar enjoyed music and sports, but was a persistently mediocre student. It was during his second year at Preah Sihanouk in 1945 that Cambodia experienced the jolting change that even an immature, disinterested student such as Sar could not help but notice. Japanese forces arrested French government officials and Cambodia was declared an independent nation. With the internment of the French, the colleges lost most of their teachers, and were closed for an extended period.

Independence didn't last, of course. With the defeat of Japan and Germany, the French moved back in. Sihanouk signed an agreement providing for the resumption of French rule, but with Cambodian autonomy. Independence was off the table for the moment, but the idea was not out of mind for a growing number of Cambodians. These major political shifts may have been jolting to the citizens of Cambodia, but seemed to have little effect on Saloth Sar at the time.

Ho Chi Minh, and his Indochinese Communist Party, had begun moving cadres into eastern Cambodia to establish bases and control, but few comprehended the significance of what was taking place in those remote jungles. That fact would change dramatically in coming years, but to a young Saloth Sar such goings-on may as well have been on the moon.

Whether it was due to growing maturity, or simply deciding it was time to apply himself, in the summer of 1947 Sar finally passed the end-of-year exam and was admitted to the Lycée Sisowath—no small accomplishment. A year later, he and two friends took the brevet, the exam to gain admission to the upper classes of the Lycée—once again, Sar failed it. With few options remaining open to him, he gained admission to the Technical School at Russey Keo in the suburbs of Phnom Penh.

It was here that Sar's academic fortunes took a turn for the better. Each year, the school offered three scholarships for continuing engineering studies at French colleges, but this year there were to be five. Sar dedicated himself, obtained his brevet, and won one of the scholarships. He was headed for college in Paris.

As his life and events unfolded, one can only wonder what the fate of Cambodia might have been had Saloth Sar failed to obtain that scholarship, as he had failed to do so many times before. For it was during his student years in Paris that Saloth Sar first began to develop his political beliefs. And though the name change didn't occur for years, it was in Paris where the metamorphosis from Saloth Sar to Pol Pot began.

The culture shock that Sar and his fellow Cambodian students likely experienced on October 1, 1949, when they stepped off the train in Paris, perhaps can best be compared to the feelings experienced by Dorothy and her friends when they first set foot inside the Emerald City, in the movie *The Wizard of Oz*. The students had, of course, been in Phnom Penh, which was somewhat multi-cultural and they spent some time in Saigon in transit to Paris.

Nothing could have prepared them for the grandeur of The City of Light. The Eiffel Tower, the Louvre, the brooding Bastille, broad boulevards, Notre Dame and its magnificence, grand architecture, all the achievements of Western Civilization were on display and available within walking distance of class. Without question, these jarring cultural excesses influenced Sar and his friends, but in different ways.

The quiet, smiling boy who left his fishing village on the banks of the Sen arrived in a post-World War II Paris that was awakening after the years of Nazi occupation, a Paris that was a throbbing hotbed of sensuality. Be-bop was the rage. Intense boys with slicked-back hair took intense, pouty-lipped girls to smoke-filled basements, talking intensely of "essence" and "existentialism" over pounding music. Arguments surged over the merits of pure Marxism over Socialism, raging into the muting light of a new dawn.

Paris in 1950 was considered to be the cultural epicenter by artists and intellectuals. Drawn by fine restaurants, and by a tolerance for experimentation in everything from music, philosophy and politics to sexuality and lifestyles, they migrated there by the thousands after the war. The "Left Bank of the Seine" became synonymous for the leftist policies of Socialism, Marxism and Communism that were fervently argued and promoted by students determined to remake the world. For Saloth Sar, it was a time of disorienting change. But it was politics, not the sensuality that was post-war Paris, that ultimately transformed Sar from an overwhelmed, indifferent student to a possessed tyrant, destined to destroy his country.

Ironically, on the day that Sar and his friends first arrived in Paris, Mao Tse Tung, standing at the Gate of Heavenly Peace in Beijing, announced the beginning of his new Chinese People's Republic. Many of Sar's fellow students in Paris were eventually swept up in the pronouncements of Mao Tse Tung.

The Cold War was in full swing, and the world was dividing into two camps—Communist forces aligned with the Soviet Union and Communist China, and countries aligned with the Western powers of America and Europe. These forces were once again at war, on the barren peninsula of Korea.

Anti-Colonialism was rampant in the South Pacific and Indochina, with Burma, India, Indonesia, and the Philippines all struggling to free themselves. In North Vietnam, Ho Chi Minh and his Viet Minh forces refused to openly associate themselves with Communism and disingenuously presented themselves as simple nationalists, fighting for independence for their country.

Without doubt the lost glory of Angkor, as they had been taught about it in school, affected Sar and the other Cambodian students. The ideal of returning Cambodia to that former glory was an incubator for national independence and established a dream in the minds of idealistic youth of being the agents to bring their country back to its former greatness.

It was in this light that Sar and his fellow Cambodians in Paris saw themselves: patriots zealous to find a way to free their country from French oppression. Independence was their only objective. How best to accomplish that goal, when neither they nor their country had the resources to do so, was the sole issue of the many hours spent in discussions and arguments in the City of Light where Marx once lived, the *Communist Manifesto* routinely read, and where the French Communist Party was the largest political party in the country. The outcome was essentially pre-ordained.

Endless arguments over how to best achieve independence for their country raged among those students. Some looked to the passive resistance of India in gaining independence from Britain. Others looked eastward at the military success of Mao Tse Tung in driving out Chiang Kai Shek and the free Chinese, and at the armed conflict of Ho Chi Minh against the French in Vietnam. Over time, a consensus formed that armed conflict was the only viable path. With the Communist governments of China and the Soviet Union now recognizing the government of Ho Chi Minh in Vietnam, it appeared to the students that the Communists were the only game in town.

Saloth Sar was slow to join that group but finally started down the irreversible path toward becoming a full-fledged Communist, although he did not admit to being one for many years. Surprisingly, it was not the *Communist Manifesto* that most influenced him. Rather, it was an obscure, seven-hundred-plus-page analysis of the French Revolution of 1789, and its attendant Terror, that established the essence of Sar's core beliefs and remained with him throughout his life. From that tome, Sar discovered his real goal in life—revolution. It was from this realization that the goal of independence could come only through revolution that the script that was to become the drama of the Khmer Rouge first began to take shape.

Alongside his conviction that revolution was the only viable path to Cambodian independence, two other principles came out of Sar's years in Paris that influenced him for the remainder of his years: First, he came to understand that the essence of Communism was class warfare between a "ruling elite" and the industrial working class, and armed revolution was the only way for the latter to overthrow the former. Second, the lessons of the French Revolution taught him that the elite rulers of a country had to be sacrificed for the greater good. The fact that Cambodia was virtually one hundred per-cent agrarian peasantry, with no "industrial working class," never seemed to register with Sar. But sacrificing the elite for the common good? That would pose no problem—just round them up and kill them all.

In January, 1953, Saloth Sar returned home from his formative "coming of age" years in Paris. In some perverse sense of twisted logic, Cambodia's "Prince of Darkness" had set his future course in the City of Light. He came home to a nation already embroiled in political turmoil and scattered armed conflicts. It would take another twenty-two years for his dreams of revolution to come to fruition, but the die had been cast.

Two years after Saloth Sar returned to his native land, another son was born in Kampong Chhnang, barely forty miles as the crow flies from Prek Sbauv. On April 17, 1975, the paths of these two Cambodian sons crossed, in what was to become one of the darkest chapters of evil ever witnessed by humankind.

Section III
Years Of Darkness

Chapter 5

Barefoot Journey Into Hell

...the light has come into the world, and men loved darkness rather than light, because their deeds were evil.

John 3:19

The old plane touched down at the Phnom Penh airport with an impatient jolt. Albert Cheng's first airplane ride was over. As the plane taxied to its parking area, the broiling midday sun quickly turned the air inside putrid and unbearable. The white and blue uniforms pushed past Albert and out the large cargo doors, their owners anxious to get into fresh air. Albert extricated himself from his spot on the fuselage floor and joined them, blinking against the bright sunlight. He nodded a thank you to the pilot, who ignored him and went on about his business. Finding an available cyclo—basically, a rickshaw on a bicycle frame—outside the terminal, he seated himself for the ride and gave his "cabbie" the address to what was to be his new home while he attended college. His new life as an independent young man, a college student no less, was about to begin.

His train trips with his brothers and sisters to Phnom Penh as he grew up had prepared him for the constant noise and confusion of the large city, the crowded streets and marketplaces, the pushing and shoving of the crowds. None of that was unexpected—but he never really grew accustomed to it. As the cyclo peddler worked his way through snarled traffic toward the house of Albert's sister, where he was to stay, he was already growing homesick and missing his days and nights spent with family, and in the jungle with Uncle Hank.

One constant in Albert's personality as he grew up was the need for, and constant searching for, a sense of peace and serenity. His family life and his trips to the jungle largely satisfied that hunger, and he often thought of his childhood as "a joyful time, a peaceful time."

Yet, there lay within Albert's personality another facet, one quite inconsistent with his description of his childhood. Quiet, peaceful Albert was also somewhat of an adventurer.

"Yes, I liked adventure," he said of his childhood days. "I wasn't what you would call wild, or anything like that, but I did like to go places, do things. I think that is another reason why I liked the trips to the jungle with Uncle Hank so much. They were always filled with strange things, lots of adventures for a small boy."

That sense of adventure was manifested in a completely unexpected way, as Albert moved into his teenage years. As conflicts between the growing bands of Khmer Rouge guerrillas and the government forces of Lon Nol grew more frequent and heated, Albert decided he wanted to go to military school.

Those years that Albert remembers as a time of peacefulness, of serene, pleasant times with family and school and meditation in the jungle with Uncle Hank, were primarily from his earlier childhood. As he matured into his teenage years that was obviously changing, not just for Cambodia but for all of Southeast Asia.

Various factions were at war with each other in Cambodia virtually non-stop from the end of World War II to the fall of the Khmer Rouge in 1979, and as Albert grew up fire-fights would erupt occasionally in the areas where he lived.

Clandestine cells of resident Communists—the "Red Khmers" (Khmer being the traditional name for Cambodians, and rouge the French word for "red") as Sihanouk had originally called them—growing out of the recruiting efforts of Pol Pot and the others from Paris were increasing in numbers and boldness. Lon Nol, having assumed control of the government when Sihanouk had fled to exile in Communist China, found his army being attacked by these guerilla groups with increasing frequency and ferocity.

"Freedom Fighters" once again found themselves at war. This time, however, they were fighting not for freedom from the French but the bands of Khmer Rouge spreading throughout the country.

From Albert's birth in 1955 until he was an early teen, the East-West struggle over Indochina had intensified, and was reaching a boiling point. In those early years, Sihanouk had been pulled in both directions, to align Cambodia either with the Communist forces of the Soviets and China, or with the Americans who were becoming increasingly insistent that he turn westward. During that time, the Vietnamese forces of Ho Chi Minh were steadily encroaching into eastern Cambodia, gaining ever-increasing footholds in the country.

Sihanouk had made his fateful decision, aligning himself with China and the Communists, a decision that infuriated the pro-West forces. In 1970, Sihanouk was forcibly overthrown by Lon Nol, the man who had at one time been his strongman and Chief of Police. Sihanouk fled into exile in China, where he was made the—

perhaps titular—head of a growing Khmer Rouge organization. The battle for Cambodia's heart and soul was on.

Parents have a way of trying to protect their children, not just from immediate physical harm but from anxiety, as well. It is difficult to imagine that the guerilla raids that disrupted travel and killed villagers could have gone unnoticed by the parents of Albert Cheng. Surely, they must have talked quietly at night, after the children were asleep, of their premonitions, their worries and fears. Surely they must have comprehended the storms that were beginning to unleash their fury on Cambodia, and wondered about their safety and future.

Those concerns and apprehensions may have been transmitted to the children of the Cheng household but regardless, boys seem to want to be soldiers. Perhaps it is part of the human genetic structure. Perhaps it is the lure of adventure. For whatever reason, in 1970, when Albert was fifteen, he decided that he wanted to join the *Ecole Militaire Enfants de Troupe*, a military school conducted by the Cambodian government. It could best be compared to our ROTC, the Reserve Officer Training Corps, where students receive schooling in various military subjects.

Obviously, he did so with his parents' approval. He would not have, could not have, done so otherwise. The class was offered once a week, but he had to also participate in training exercises with the Cambodian military forces in the area. If Albert joined to get some adventure, he got his wish. Twice.

"One time, I was riding on a truck at the rear of a convoy hauling medical supplies and food from Battambang to Pursat. Up ahead a ways, at the head of the convoy, a flash and large explosion shocked us as an RPG barely missed one of the trucks. We had been ambushed by the Khmer Rouge forces. Suddenly, swarms of these black uniforms came out of the jungle, firing their

AK-47s. We ducked under the trucks for cover. Very quickly, it turned into a real fire-fight with our troops firing their M-16s in defense. It lasted for what seemed like about an hour and a half, before the Khmer Rouge gave up and disappeared back into the jungle. I didn't feel like I was under any real danger, but it was scary," Albert confessed.

Albert had little to say about his parents' reaction to his "adventure," but they apparently accepted it as Albert was allowed to continue in the military classes. But that didn't last. A second time was one time too many for Albert's mother.

"The second time we were ambushed was at night, and we barely held them off. My mother told me enough is enough, and that she never wanted to see me wear the military uniform or carry a weapon again.

"Of course, I honored my mother and did what she asked. I never touched a rifle again. But that is why my parents decided to send me to Phnom Penh to go to school—the fighting was getting too close.

"I didn't really mind," Albert added. "I didn't really want to fight my own countrymen. So that is when I left home." After a pause, he added, "Of course, that was the last time I ever saw my parents."

So, Albert's leaving home for Phnom Penh was more than simply finishing what we would call high school, and leaving for college. His search for adventure had proved more successful than his parents were willing to accept, and it was apparent that they were becoming aware of the growing threats from the Khmer Rouge. The fighting could no longer be glossed over, far less ignored.

Albert made the trip to Phnom Penh in that beat up, beef-hauling cargo plane for the simple reason that both the railroad and

National Highway 5—which would have been the road on which the ambushes experienced by Albert had occurred—had been cut and mined by the Khmer Rouge. To have attempted that trip by land would obviously have been near-suicidal.

For the three years that Albert was in Phnom Penh, most of the fighting was well away from the capital. In many respects, for a student immersed in college-level courses, the fighting would have been "out of sight and out of mind." During these years, the military of Cambodia, Lon Nol's forces, grew increasingly brutal and repressive. They fought with determination—or perhaps desperation—but the Khmer Rouge forces were achieving critical mass in their attempt to overthrow the Lon Nol government.

Supported logistically by the Chinese, their ranks swelling daily by peasants infuriated by American B-52 bombers carpet-bombing their country, the Khmer Rouge were becoming unstoppable. Village by village, Lon Nol's forces were pushed back toward the capital. And as each new village came under assault, thousands more refugees poured into a swollen Phnom Penh that had no room for them. It was a disaster in the making.

January 1, 1975, was the beginning of the end. Tens of thousands of Khmer Rouge had surrounded the capital. In the early morning hours, not long after midnight, an intense bombardment of the outer defense perimeter of Phnom Penh was begun. For hours, the earth shook and bright flashes lit the horizon as rockets and artillery shells rained down on the edges of the city. As morning dawned, city dwellers looked across the Mekong at the acrid smoke of burning buildings and fuel stores.

Refugees who had fled their villages to escape the fighting, who had sought safety in the biggest city in their country, had once again come under bombardment. Simple village peasants, scared, confused, dazed, desperate, wounded or perhaps dying from the night-long pounding, pushed from the outskirts farther into the center of the city amid rubble and destruction that was to become commonplace.

For three and a half months the devastation continued, the destruction worsened, and the suffering deepened as the noose tightened. People crowded ever more densely into a shrinking center of the city. Then, on the night of April 16, came the final blow. Rockets, mortars and artillery of the Khmer Rouge could now reach the city's center and a night-long nightmarish pounding began.

It was a scene straight out of Dante's *Inferno*. Buildings exploding in thundering blasts, debris raining down on the streets. An eerie whistling of a shell, a stunning blast, the earth shaking. Chunks of plaster falling from ceilings, dust puffing out of cracks and settling on furniture being jostled about the floor. Windows breaking, glass tinkling on floors, screams of the scared and wounded mingling with the distraught wailing of dogs trembling and cowering in corners, too frightened to move. A constant whup-whup-whupping of helicopters strafing enemy positions blending with the rattle of distant machine gun fire, incendiary tracers tying the gunship to the earth like a tether. Panic-stricken soldiers of Lon Nol, being pushed steadily backward, dropping their weapons, fleeing for their lives. Hour after relentless hour, the apocalypse rained without mercy, the city and its people being torn apart.

Like a tranquil sunrise after a night of terrorizing thunderstorms, morning broke eerily silent, the sky bright and clear. The death certificate for Phnom Penh had been written and executed. April 17, 1975, saw the sun rising on a crushed and defeated city. Lon Nol's forces were fleeing in panic as Khmer Rouge troops poured into the center of Phnom Penh.

Much is known about the fall of Phnom Penh. Pictures taken by the few reporters who stayed to the end were published world-wide, movies were made, books were written. There is much factual information from that time, but what of the emotion? What was it like for a young college student when the city fell? What was it like, surviving a night in which your world is being blown apart, and watching the Khmer Rouge soldiers enter your city?

"I remember, I had returned from class to the temple, as usual," Albert recalled, hesitating a bit before answering.

He had, when he first arrived in Phnom Penh, stayed with his sister, Ty, at her house. But later on he had moved into a room at a temple. There was nothing unusual about doing that, as the temples were always open to those looking for a place to stay.

"At that point...rockets and mortars...began pounding the city," Albert continued. "That was a horrible time...I began seeing people blown to pieces, bloodshed, screaming, yelling. I remember the carnage, the smell of blood everywhere. All day, all night, it never stopped. Military helicopters flew along the Mekong River, shooting, constantly shooting. At that time I began to feel the closeness of the battleground. When the sun set, I didn't know what to do. I lay down and tried to sleep. The rockets kept coming...just non-stop, sometimes they threw my whole body off the bed, tossed it up...I was very scared, and couldn't sleep at all. And by the morning...the whole capital was covered by these black uniforms."

The word "black" was emphasized with an intensity, a ferocity, that was unsettling. It is well known that the Khmer Rouge all dressed in black shirts and shorts, or pants, and all wore sandals made from slabs of tire treads. From what little is known about that choice of "uniform," it was apparently purely utilitarian. Dyed using the berries of local plants, the black color made everybody blend together—lack of status seemed to be crucial to Communist theology—and didn't show the grime. There seemed to be no intentional "Darth Vader" element to that choice of color, no thought given to the psychological effect their appearance must have had on the people. But intentional or not, the effect was chilling for those who experienced it first hand.

"The Cambodia Republic, the Freedom Fighters, they all withdrew back into the capital," Albert continued. "I saw M-16s and M-79s all over the streets, all over the place, where soldiers dropped them...running for their lives. Those who had more information about the Khmer Rouge...they would tell the soldiers, 'Take off your uniforms, put on civilian clothes, right away, or they will kill you.' While I was in the temple, the Khmer Rouge...all in black. I can't even look at their eyes. They killed all the monks, just shot them, and piled up their bodies."

Much has been made of the events of April 17, 1975, in Phnom Penh when it fell to the rag-tag soldiers of the Khmer Rouge. Enormous contrast existed that day between the chaos and destruction borne of the final assault, versus the celebration of the "victory" as the troops came pouring into the city. Pictures from that day show both elements in graphic detail. There are the pictures of burning cars and buildings, bodies of the dead and dying lying scattered about, retreating soldiers of the national army running for their lives. But other pictures show joyous residents celebrating as armored vehicles, as well as co-opted civilian vehicles, all laden with victorious, black-clad soldiers came parading down city streets.

For many Cambodians, the fighting that had been taking place for the previous two years or more was in essence a civil war. Although the people were by their nature loyal to their king, Sihanouk had been exiled to China and was supporting the Khmer

Rouge. Lon Nol, who had deposed the king, was corrupt in his own way and viewed by many as nothing more than an extension of Sihanouk, who was no more than a lackey of the French. Lon Nol had become increasingly oppressive as he fought for his political life.

A general belief existed that the Khmer Rouge were fighting to overthrow the Lon Nol government in order to establish independence, and a true democracy in Cambodia. One of the best kept secrets of the war at that time, however, was that the Khmer Rouge leaders were Communists, through and through. Pol Pot didn't openly admit his Communist affiliation for nearly a year after Phnom Penh had fallen.

Strangely enough, at least initially there was much rejoicing in the city. In spite of the carnage and bloodshed—perhaps even in spite of rumors that might have been floating about regarding these strange-looking child-soldiers wearing their black shorts and shirts and tire-slab sandals who came pouring into the streets of the city—it was all over. The war had ended. The fighting would cease, and there could be a return to normal life. There would be peace. People poured into the streets to celebrate and welcome the victorious soldiers.

It was reminiscent of pictures from liberated cities of Europe in the waning days of World War II. Adults cheered and tossed flowers to the soldiers, as a bizarre sort of "victory parade" spontaneously erupted throughout the streets of the city. Children climbed up on the bedraggled assortment of "military" vehicles, many of which were nothing more than old trucks with weapons mounted in the back.

It was not long, however, after the "victory parades" that it became apparent there was not to be peace. Euphoria soon evaporated, as a vague sense of unease quickly began to infiltrate the city. People were not prepared for the crude, primitive nature of the "troops" invading their city. Many of the "soldiers" were teenagers, many no more than twelve or thirteen years old, girls and boys alike. Many of them had spent essentially their whole lives deep in the jungles, and appeared to have no concept of life in civilized environments, a life that included toilets and personal hygiene.

But it was not the primitive behavior or disheveled appearance, nor the shoddy, dirty black uniforms and tire-tread sandals that most alarmed the populace. Rather, it was the cold, unfeeling stare of eyes that seemed devoid of human feelings. In those eyes was a sullen anger at the people who had lived in comfort while they— the true redeemers and reformers of Cambodia who had endured the bombing raids of Lon Nol—had struggled to survive in the jungle with little to eat.

Over time, they developed a resentment that had metamorphosed into an irrational, deep-seated hatred for the cities and all that urban life represented. They were determined to eliminate that disparity, that injustice. Killing the guilty, ridding the country of its cesspools of iniquity, was a duty they accepted with apparent relish.

"I could not look in the eye of the soldier," Albert repeated on several occasions, as he talked about those early hours under the forces of Pol Pot. "They looked so cold. They just look at you, and shoot you if you don't do what they say."

The eventual fate of the country, the true meaning of the fall of the city, had little to do with that scene of joyful celebration taking place the morning of April 17, 1975. The coming fate of Cambodia and its people had been decided long before, in crude thatch-roofed huts in the jungles of northeast Cambodia. There, a small, mysterious, secretive group met with its leader, Pol Pot, and agreed on a plan for the country, once the Lon Nol government had been overthrown.

During his years of study at college in Paris, and the later years establishing relationships with Communist China and the leaders of North Vietnam, Pol Pot had come to a decision. Cambodia was to be returned to its former glory and greatness as a nation—the "lost glory of Angkor Wat" would be re-established, the country recreated in a new pure form, rid of all outside influences. All forms of Western culture were evil and corrupt, Pol Pot believed, and hence must be cleansed from the country. Cambodia could not be returned to its once glorious stature until, and unless, it was "purified" of such influences.

Pol Pot was aware from his studies in Paris that the Communist revolutions of the Soviets and China were predicated on the industrial "working classes." He was also acutely aware that Cambodia had no such "working class." The vast majority of Cambodians were rice farmers and peasants, most of whom lived subsistence lives of poverty. Virtually all technical and professional positions in the country were held by Vietnamese, because far too few Cambodians had the education and skills required for such positions.

Pol Pot did not see this as a problem. In his mind, only the Cambodian peasant represented the true, the pure, Cambodia. The new People's Republic of Kampuchea would be cleansed. Cambodians hated the Vietnamese, so ridding the country of them would be an improvement. Cambodians corrupted by the West would either be "reformed," or "removed." Sitting in crude huts buried in the jungle, this small band that was to lead Cambodia into its nightmare of insanity concluded that Cambodia as it presently existed consisted of three classes of people.

First, there were the "true" Cambodians, the simple rice farmer, the peasant who led a glorified life of tilling the soil, of earning his living through the hard labor of his own efforts. This idealized peasant was the foundation on which a new Kampuchea would rise. Such an idealized view ignored, of course, the reality of the grinding poverty and harsh lives of many of those peasants, of the poisonous snakes and leeches in the rice paddies, of the hours of stoop labor under a punishing sun which were required to plant and harvest that rice. Nevertheless, that life was to become the new "Nirvana."

Then, there were the "new people." These were the Cambodians who had been corrupted by the influence of Capitalism and Western Culture, but who could still be "salvaged." They would be forcibly removed from the cities and converted to peasant status, working alongside the true, the pure Cambodians to build the new Kampuchea. They would learn the benefits of hard labor and self-sacrifice, they would experience the joy of earning one's own way through the tilling of the soil, of being part of the cycle of life in the rice fields.

Finally, there were the "unsalvageable", those who had been so corrupted by the West that they could not possibly be redeemed. They were beyond salvation, and had to be "removed," the country cleansed of their corrupting influence.

And who were these "unsalvageable" citizens, these fellow Cambodians who were the dross of the new society who were to be discarded like so much garbage, whose only value was as fertilizer in the rice fields? They were the ones who might show any sign of being educated, of being "Westernized." Soft hands, free of calluses, meant a life of living off others, of never toiling in the fields. To wear glasses was a sure sign of having had one's sight degraded by years of study, of becoming educated. Any government official was tainted by the corrupt government. Any trace of a French accent? It had to have been born of years of schooling under French tutelage. A large vocabulary? Another sure sign of being educated. All such corrupting influences could not be allowed to poison the new Kampuchea. The fate of any such person was sealed in the jungles, long before those unknowing people paraded in the streets in celebration of the "victory."

A poignant, and personal, side note to this inhumane and bizarre plan, was Albert's father's situation. As an employee of the Sihanouk and Lon Nol governments, trained by French officials, educated and middle class, his death warrant was signed long before he had any comprehension of what was to become of his country and his family. Of course, in the twisted logic of the Khmer Rouge leaders, if the father was corrupted, then ipso facto, so must be the family. All must die. Albert lost his mother and father, two sisters and a brother, all victims of such depraved insanity. The family members who did survive, including Albert, did so only by deception, by dressing as peasants and assuming different names.

Albert never learned where his parents were when Phnom Penh fell, or what became of them. Khmer Rouge troops entered Battambang on April 18, 1975, and promptly rounded up military leaders, under the ruse of needing them to help train new troops "to drive the tanks." Those who were thus captured were hauled off into fields and executed. Battambang was forcibly evacuated a day later. Whether his parents were still in Pursat, and if so what became of them, will never be known.

To accomplish this transformation of a country, all citizens were to be evacuated from Phnom Penh—as well as from all the major cities—and moved into the countryside where they were to be catalogued, sorted, indexed and marked. The "New People" would be relocated to join the peasants in the rice fields, learning the glories of the agrarian life. The others were to be eliminated. Thus it was that soon after the fall of Phnom Penh began one of the most bizarre episodes in modern times. The city, flooded by then to a population approaching two million by the refugees who had previously fled from the fighting in the countryside, was emptied—turned into a ghost town.

"The Khmer Rouge set up 'interview' camps," Albert vividly remembered. "The Communists told people, 'Our new government will need educated people to help run it.' It was a trap...to get people to confess to being elite, educated. In Phnom Penh, I saw people, professors, educated, doctors, teachers, government workers, they all signed their names to help. Then that evening, I was down by the Mekong River...I saw these same people, all tied up."

Albert paused, staring out the windows at scenes he had spent thirty years trying to forget.

"The Khmer Rouge walked them down to river...they shot them all. Killed them. Tossed the bodies in the river. From that point on, I never trusted anything, never talked to anyone."

In the first few days after the fall of the city, several hundred government officials, politicians and police were rounded up and brutally executed, their bodies tossed in hurriedly dug mass graves or in the Mekong River. However, in spite of the fact that many people died in those early days, there was no widespread immediate mass extermination. That came later.

Horrible as the scenes described by Albert were, they are not the scenes that are the most perplexing about the fall of Phnom Penh. That story began three days after the fall of the city. Simply told, in a matter of hours, Phnom Penh stood vacant, empty of all life. The "why" of that circumstance, of Pol Pot's determination to transform Cambodia into an agrarian society free of all Western influence, is well documented. What isn't so obvious is the "how" of that event. It was one thing for Khmer Rouge troops to be able to empty a small village in the jungle. Often, they would just summon the village leader and execute him in front of the villagers, telling them they must leave or they would also be executed. Little time was wasted as the villagers fled for their lives.

But Phnom Penh was a large city, many square miles in area. It is far more difficult to comprehend more than a million people suddenly disrupting their lives and leaving the city—just "getting out of Dodge."

When asked how on earth the Khmer Rouge got everyone to just grab up a few pots and pans, perhaps a little rice, and simply start walking out of town, some not even taking time to lock the doors on their homes, Albert looked as though we Americans were simply too naïve to understand the people who destroyed his home. As it turned out, the approach was no different except in scale from that used on the villagers in the jungle.

"They turned their AK-47s on us, shooting above our heads," he explained, rather emphatically. "They yelled, 'Just go. Go! Leave!' If someone didn't obey…they just shot them. Dead bodies were all over the place.

"And that's how I decided to just…run off," he added, reflecting on that chaotic and frightening time in his life.

An attempt was made in the movie *The Killing Fields* to depict the evacuation of Phnom Penh, but didn't seem to do justice to the reality of it. In the movie, thousands of people began walking slowly—and rather passively—out of town along one of the broad avenues. It all appeared quite… scripted, and orderly.

But from all accounts, the evacuation was a disorganized exercise in panic and chaos. Parents screaming for children lost in the crowd, terrified children screaming for parents, people trying to push bicycles loaded with all the possessions that could be quickly tied on, pots and pans clanking on the backs of people turned into oxen. Pushing, shoving, panic-stricken, terrified of cold-eyed "soldiers" scarcely taller than the AK-47s they brandished who constantly threatened them, images of family members shot down in front of their eyes burning in their minds, the exodus soon assumed the characteristics of lava. It did not flow. It oozed, with progress barely discernible for hours, or even days, at a time.

No one was immune, no one exempted. Regardless of their condition, all patients were evacuated from hospitals, being rolled on gurneys if necessary and pushed along the streets. Soldiers missing legs, or perhaps innocent victims of the fighting, struggled to hobble or scoot their way along with the crowd. Elderly, too frail to walk, were propped up or carried by family, or left to die along the way. Pregnant women, newborn babies, all had to leave, however they might do that. No one was left to "run the city," as there was nothing left operating that required someone to run it.

The term "Khmer Rouge" is often used as though it was a single entity, a tightly organized military unit similar to the armies of developed nations. There was a chain of command, of sorts. Pol Pot and his small cadre were the unquestioned leaders of the group but at the field level there was considerable disorganization, and competition for supremacy over areas of control. In many respects it was not unlike Afghanistan with its many warlords. Without doubt, each local leader wanted to do things his way, in his area of operation.

Thus it was that the evacuees of Phnom Penh were pulled in several directions. Much of the city was pushed to the north and west, along National Highway 5 toward Battambang. Other groups headed southwest toward the Gulf of Thailand, still others east and southeast. In the months and years to come, that would result in far different fates for those involved. Many of the worst of the atrocities occurred in the regions of the north and west. Treatment of those who went southwest, or southeast, seemed to be less inhumane.

Once the bulk of the population was on the move, the next obvious issue arose. The Khmer Rouge had made no plans, had no provisions, for dealing with the chaos they had created. What do you do with several hundred thousand people who have little or no food, no water, no place to spend the nights, no toilets? Within hours, the evacuation bogged down, came to a sluggish halt. By the end of the third day, the mass which was migrating northward had moved at most five miles.

Albert was talking one afternoon about that forced march. He was at one end of a long hallway in our church that approached the length of a football field, talking about the evacuation and how it had become bogged down.

"In one day, we moved maybe down there," he said, nodding toward the end of that hallway. "We just went nowhere."

April is the dry season in Cambodia, and the hottest month. It is near the equator. It gets hot—broiling, sweltering, brain-melting hot. As the sun steamed the stagnant mass of humanity, dehydration and heat stroke began to take their inexorable toll. Babies became listless, their faces flushed, as mothers sought some form of shade for them. People had little to drink or eat, and were becoming dehydrated, beginning to starve.

The sick and elderly began dying along the way. There was no way to bury the dead. Bodies were left to rot and decay where they fell, alongside the growing piles of personal belongings being discarded. The stench and pall of death hung heavily over people who were losing the capacity to mourn. Pots, pans, household goods, personal belongings, piles of clothes intermingled with the dead and dying.

Of course, that was not unacceptable to the Khmer Rouge leaders. The new Cambodia, the new Kampuchea, could not be built on the backs of the weak, the sick and elderly. They were expendable, the country better off without them. Their deaths simply meant more rice for the productive.

Another contributor to the slow pace was the "interviews." In keeping with the plan for new Kampuchea, it was essential that people be categorized. Thus, along the way, interview stations were set up. One by one, people were required to create their "biography," to present, in detail, their background. Where are you from? What did you do? Who were your parents? Where did you go to school? Notes were made of identifying characteristics. Did they wear glasses, or speak with good vocabulary—sure signs of an advanced education? Did they work for the government, or in a technical field?

Meticulous records were kept, as one by one those with peasant backgrounds, the "true" Khmer, were separated from those who were to become the "new people," and those who were expendable. Deceit was the tool of the trade, with the usual ruse being to tell the people that skilled, educated people would be needed to train the new Cambodia, or that government leaders were needed to help in the cities.

Many fell into the trap and volunteered, offering their assistance. Their patriotism, or generosity, sealed their fate. Most of those were bound together and blindfolded, led off into the scrub underbrush and executed, bludgeoned to death, asphyxiated, beheaded, or killed by whatever means of extermination or tools at hand suited the executioner at the moment. They weren't worth wasting a bullet, so were seldom shot. Sometimes the bodies were buried, but often were left to rot or were thrown into ponds or rice paddies. Rumors ran rampant through the masses, and people discarded eye glasses, rubbed dirt on their clothes, changed their names and lied about their careers, education and background in desperate attempts to survive.

It was in this time of chaos, fear and panic that Albert realized that he had to escape, had to run away from the madness. Somehow, he managed to escape undetected from the crowds and struck out on his own. Given the Khmer Rouge's fanatical intention to control the population, it was a surprise that Albert had been able to simply "run off." By the same token, given the mass chaos of the time it is possible to see how anyone sufficiently determined—or desperate—could have "slipped through the cracks."

"I wanted to go west," he explained, when asked where he headed. "There was a book, someone wrote a book about the journey to the west. Someone, whoever the author was, said it is time to head west, to escape to Thailand. But I wanted to take the National Road 5, to go to Pursat, to see if I could see my family. I headed for Kampong Chhnang."

That was a choice likely born more of stress and the emotions of the time than from rationality. Highway 5 had long been too dangerous to travel, resulting in his airplane ride years earlier. Then too, by that time National Highway 5 was being turned into a parking lot for people. Of the two million people who were forced out of Phnom Penh, it is likely that at least half were pushed northward, many of them up that highway. It is not difficult to imagine that one traveling alone could have skirted all that, undetected. Albert's plan, however, didn't pan out.

"I talked to a farmer along the way," Albert explained, "and he told me I should not go there (toward Kampong Chhnang). It was under the control of the Khmer Rouge, and everywhere there were mines, minefields everywhere. So I changed my direction, and headed east, to Kampong Thom." Ironically, in doing so Albert likely passed near Prek Sbauv, the birthplace village of Pol Pot.

That choice of alternate route raised some questions, as the area had to be crawling with Khmer Rouge soldiers. Traveling through there would surely have been quite risky.

"Oh, they were all over the place," Albert agreed, rather emphatically. "At that time, I had to travel mostly at night. I began to know the period of time when they rested, and that would be the time for me to keep on moving."

His route also seemed antithetical to his goal of trying to get to Thailand, as Kampong Thom is on the east side of the great lake of Tonle Sap, and north along the road to Siem Reap. It would have been much farther to the Thai border to the north, than to the west. But the border to the west lay across the lake.

As Albert told of what turned out to be his first of two attempts to escape to Thailand, it took some effort to comprehend the stark reality of that desperate journey. First, there was the simple issue of distance. It is approximately 175 miles from Phnom Penh to the historic temple of Angkor Wat, at least another seventy-five miles from there to Battambang, then another seventy-five miles to the Thai border—a total distance of well over three hundred miles.

Imagine deciding to take a walk, say, across the length of Oklahoma, or Kansas. Oh, yes. One other thing. You have no food and no money with which to buy any, and just the clothes you were wearing when you were forced at gunpoint out of Phnom Penh. You have no protection from the weather. It is April in Cambodia, the hottest and driest time of the year. You have no water or means of carrying any. You must eat what you can find—insects, frogs, rats, anything you can catch.

There is but one hard-surfaced road from Phnom Penh, through Kampong Thom, to Siem Reap, the large town nearest to the temple at Angkor Wat—and it is crawling with Khmer Rouge soldiers who want to capture or kill you. So you must travel cross country, through rice fields, woods, jungle, whatever lies between you and safety. Of course, the trip must be made entirely at night, and you have no light and couldn't risk turning it on, anyway. Villages, where food and shelter might be found, cannot be risked because of the threat of Khmer Rouge being there.

This was the reality faced by Albert as he made his way northward. But having given up on heading west, was it still his plan to get to Thailand?

"Oh yes, I was still trying to get to Thailand. But I remembered one of my teachers, and a picture he showed us of Angkor Wat, so I decided to try to get to Angkor Wat," Albert explained.

Angkor Wat, now the number one tourist attraction in Cambodia, is as hard to describe as it is to put in context. It was an engineering marvel, the largest city in Southeast Asia during the centuries of Khmer supremacy, and the center of all Buddhist religious activity. "Angkor" means city and "wat," of course, is Cambodian for temple. Angkor Wat is a massive city/temple complex. It is to Cambodians what Rome might be to Italians, a city that represents everything that was great about their past—and with Vatican City, is also the heart of their religion. Now imagine Rome largely in ruins, covered with vines, lost in the jungle. Until it was restored in the 1940s, that was Angkor Wat.

The Angkor empire ruled all of Southeast Asia for hundreds of years, and Angkor Wat was its heart and soul. At its peak, Angkor Wat occupied a territory equal to all of modern New York City and had a population of at least three quarters of a million people. A massive, complex moat and canal system stored water for both personal use and farming. But as the Angkor empire faded and crumbled, Angkor Wat was abandoned to the jungle and fell into near ruin. It has been largely restored to its breathtaking original condition, and for Albert, getting to Angkor Wat was like getting to Mecca for a Muslim.

"Oh, yes!" he exclaimed, still excited by the memory of his visit to the temple. After that, he headed for Battambang, the second largest city in Cambodia and his home until he was approximately two years old.

"Yes, I wanted to get to Battambang, and then on to the border from there," he confirmed. "But that is where I got captured." He made it that far, but it was in his childhood home that his freedom came to an end. Albert had traveled nearly three hundred miles, under difficult and extremely hazardous conditions. But those days would, in the months to come, seem easy by comparison. Albert had endured a barefoot journey into Hell.

"Oh yes, I was barefooted," he insisted, "because at that time you didn't want to show anything that would make them think you are a city kind of person, anymore. Anything, everything, even your language. You must look like the villager, the peasant."

It had already become evident to most Cambodians that to be anything but a peasant was tantamount to a death sentence.

How long did the journey take? Making even four or five miles each night would have easily required six weeks, maybe more. But time as told by a calendar was an artifact of the educated, meaningless to the peasant. That fact was to become reality to Albert, indeed, had already done so.

"I assume it had to take weeks," he agreed, "but at that time, I didn't have a sense of what was Monday, Tuesday, any more. That was done. Finished. You think, okay, sunrise. Sunset. Sunrise. Sunset. And that was it. Anything else from out of the past was completely out of it.

"I didn't have the mindset of wanting to know anything," he recalled, pausing a few moments to collect himself before continuing. "It was the most shocking time, the most shocking time. Heads being cut off. The most horrible things that I see at that moment, I don't believe that my conscious mind could…how would you say it? In my mind, I could only think *What in the world am I in?*

"I remember one night, I was so tired, my body exhausted, and I couldn't find anything to drink. Along the road, I ran into this little puddle. I soaked up my scarf (his krama, the long, colorful checkered scarf often worn by many Cambodians as part of their culture) to suck on. Then, later, I ran onto this beautiful lotus pond, and I was so happy. I ran into it, and started drinking. When I had filled up my thirst, I looked closely at the lotus blossoms, at the pond…hundreds of skeletons were in that pond…no wonder the pond was so beautiful. After I had filled up my belly, and I saw all those skulls, and eyes…." He got silent for a bit, then quietly added, "That is what I went through constantly, every day."

Executions of civilians on a mass basis were only just beginning, but the Khmer Rouge had summarily dumped the bodies of government soldiers in ponds, or wherever it might be convenient, after battles. They did so not to dispose of the bodies. They weren't trying to be respectful of the dead, and could not have been less concerned about leaving the dead of their enemy to rot where they fell. They tossed them in the ponds and wells to pollute the water, and keep the enemy from being able to use it. Later, many such sites would also be filled with the bodies of civilians who had died under the extreme treatment of the Khmer

Rouge, or had been executed by them as part of their "remaking" of Cambodia.

What about food, during his trek northward, trying to get to Thailand? For Americans accustomed to a McDonald's at every interstate highway off-ramp, or pizza parlors anxious to deliver to your front door, Albert's journey was incomprehensible. Even if there were animals running loose, how would he catch them? And if so, how would he cook them? A camp fire would have been a signal in the night to your captors. Villagers could not be trusted to not turn you in, if asked for food. What was there to scavenge? How did he eat?

"Oh, my, just about anything I could grab. You know, it was the Khmer Rouge plan to move people from the city into the rice fields. So I would sometimes just sneak into them (the groups working the rice fields) to get what ever I could. I remember one time I saw a huge banana tree, and a pig eating something by the tree. I could hear it eating, just glorp, glorp, eating, eating, so I go over to see what it was eating...."

There was a long hesitation.

"It was a human being, a body. It was the corpse. The pig was eating it...I ran away."

After another long pause, the subject was changed to his age at the time of his attempted escape. His passport indicated he was born in 1959, but other records show he was born in 1955. He would have been just twenty years old.

"Nothing's exact," he agreed. "I didn't remember very much at that time. The funny thing is, when I arrived at the United Nations camp, I had completely forgotten my name, my date of birth, everything. The thing is, I had to use at least five different names. Because any name that related to the city folk...you'd be dead."

That experience was common. Once the true nature of the Khmer Rouge had become apparent, people quickly learned that any suspicion, any hint, that a person might be from the city, might be an intellectual or educated, more times than not resulted in that person being brutally killed. People adopted desperate measures to lose their old identities, to become, not so much a different person, but no person at all—a non-entity, a mindless slave laborer in the new Kampuchea.

In spite of his best efforts, in spite of surviving weeks of travel under the worst of circumstances, it was all to no avail. The day came, somewhere around Battambang, that his luck ran out.

"During all the weeks of trying to make it to Thailand, to making my escape, I had to constantly avoid the troops. They were everywhere, around all the time. I tried to avoid them, but the last day, the day that I ran into them, there was just no way out...no way out. They surrounded me.

"I just ran into them...ran into them.... It was the most frightening time...I thought, *This is the end of it. My life is over.* They surrounded me, and people scattered all over. I gave up, just gave up, because physically, I was beat up, couldn't move any longer. They blindfolded me, and took me from there.

"We were around Battambang. I recognized it. Later on, I know one of the camps we were in was near Battambang. They tied me up, and just dropped me there, with the others."

It didn't take long for Albert to be introduced to the absolute control the Khmer Rouge had over their captives. They may have been marginally insane in their plans for the country, but they were masters at mind control, of turning people into robots.

"They divided people into sections. The thing about the Communists, they are so good about dividing into groups, maybe ten in a group, so we can hardly see each other unless they need us, and then we would see each other out in the woods, or the rice fields. That is one of the ways they control us."

After many weeks of traveling barefoot, scavenging for food, with no change of clothes, traveling off the roads and paths, it would not be difficult to imagine how Albert must have appeared. Without doubt, he would have looked far more like a peasant than a "city" person. What had led the Khmer Rouge to assume that he was not just a local peasant, but one to be taken prisoner?

"I had learned by that time, you have ear, you don't want to hear. You have eye, you don't want to see. You have mouth, you don't want to talk. You know nothing. Nothing. I don't trust anything about their government, what they say," he said, sounding just as emphatic at that moment as he must have felt thirty years earlier.

But the Khmer Rouge were relentless in interviewing captives, ferreting out their past. Lies, no matter how skillfully rendered, were told in one's native accent. And one educated in French does not sound like a peasant. Your very voice testifies against you. And Albert was no different. He was now one of the millions who had become a "resource" to be utilized, less than a slave, for a slave is considered to have economic value. Captives of the Khmer Rouge were consumables, to be used until there was nothing left.

"I tried to favor them, tried to really please them. In the rice fields, I did my very best, more than the average farmer. At harvest time, they sent us out into the rice fields. Hot. Summer. Sweat. We have one of those special sickles. You lift up the rice with one part of the blade, grab it with your left hand, then use the other part of the blade to cut it off. Do that, cut it, do that, cut it. I did that over and over, and I end up smashing my finger. Almost split the whole thing. Blood just shooting. They were watching, but I just pretended nothing had happened," he related.

"Of course, they didn't give me any medical treatment, of any sort," he added. "There was no such thing as medical treatment for the captives."

The lack of medical treatment was a result of two factors. First, there were virtually no medical supplies available, anywhere in the country. Second, and far more relevant, was that whatever supplies might have been available, they would not have been wasted on one of the captives. You either survived your injury, your illness, or you died. Either way, it made no difference to them.

If you survived to work another day, then you worked another day. Work was the basis for your existence, wherever you might be needed.

"They moved us around, at different times. If they needed us up in the woods, in the mountains near the Thai border, they moved us there. Sometimes they moved us to the rice fields. Just wherever they needed labor."

Pol Pot's concept of rebuilding Cambodia into an agrarian society based on the traditional peasant, forcibly converting city dwellers into rice farmers, was not a totally new one. In 1957, as the new People's Republic of China was completing the first Five Year Plan under leader Mao Tse Tung, he concluded that China was not moving quickly enough into a self-sufficient nation.

To expedite the process, the infamous Great Leap Forward was instituted, based on the establishment of rural communes, mass migration from the cities into small villages, and on collective (forced) labor. By and large, the attempt was a colossal failure, but the project was widely known. It was much in the news in America at the time. Pol Pot was close to the Chinese leaders, and without question had to be familiar with all that was going on there.

There is little evidence, though, that Pol Pot learned much from the failures of the Great Leap Forward. In the first place, one objective of the Great Leap was a dramatic increase in steel production, and Pol Pot had already decided that the future and economy of Cambodia were to be entirely agricultural—primarily rice farming. Industrial economies, that use steel and manufacture things, were intrinsically Western and Capitalistic—and therefore evil, in the irrational mind of Pol Pot.

Given that, the national intentions of Pol Pot can at least be understood. He was, in his own way, attempting a Cambodian version of a Great Leap Forward, never mind that he was placing the nation on a one-way road to destruction and oblivion. Moving city-dwelling populations into the country to become rice farmers is at least consistent with that objective.

What is incomprehensible about the four years of Khmer Rouge rule in Cambodia was not the forced mass migration to the country, or even the forced collective labor. No, what cannot be understood or explained is the depraved obsession with brutalizing fellow citizens, ultimately reducing them to something less than animals, robbing them of their very humanity.

After the forced evacuations into the country, two themes quickly evolved. First was the extent to which sadistic brutality, torture and executions immediately became a routine part of the modus operandi of the Khmer Rouge. The more horrific the treatment, the more the captors seemed to enjoy inflicting it. Anecdotal stories abound not just of torture and executions, but of treatment that was as depraved as it was pointless. And once captured, Albert was not immune to such treatment. Long hours of forced labor in the rice fields was not enough. He had to be demeaned, treated worse than animals.

"I remember the most horrible, horrible, thing that they did to me," he related, emphasizing the word 'horrible,' "to see how I would react, to see if I am not what I said I was, even though I worked every day to do what they say. If I make them think I am educated, cannot do peasant work, I'd be dead. But the thing is, after a while I would have been glad if they chopped my head off, just been done with it. But they wouldn't do that. They just enjoyed torturing, torturing, day and night.

"Out in the rice fields, they build these squares, where people go to relieve themselves. They sent me to collect it in baskets, to carry on my shoulder, all the…what is the right word? Human… waste?"

That was commonly done in other countries. Soldiers coming home from Korea and Vietnam would talk about peasants carrying "honey buckets" to the fields.

"First, they made us cut these grasses, and mix with that what you would call…excrement? Then we had to carry it to the rice paddies…." He looked away, staring out the window for several seconds before he could continue. "That's what they did. Every day, every day…just like hell on earth. All by hand. We had to mix it, spread it in the rice field, all by hand. Then the rice had to get planted."

A second phenomenon soon developed as part of the "re-education" of the populace, and that was an obsession with mind control far beyond simple behavior control. Freedom is the natural state of man, and Communism is antithetical to freedom. One common denominator to Communist takeovers of countries is the massive, pervasive propaganda efforts. None but a small fraction of any population voluntarily subscribes to Communist principles. Most have to be brainwashed and forced to profess a belief in it. Thus it was with Pol Pot and his Khmer Rouge.

It was not sufficient to the Khmer Rouge that their captive slave laborers do the requisite work. Their personality had to be destroyed. All sense of self had to be eliminated. Nothing you had belonged to you, not even your very thoughts, because "you" don't exist.

Pol Pot refused, until late in the reign, to identify the Khmer Rouge with the Communist Party. The movement assumed an identity, known as "Angkar," which loosely translated means "highest organization." In a broad sense, the term was used in the way that we use the term "government." Soldiers in World War II were often humorously referred to as "GIs," or "government issue," intimating that the soldier was not a person but something owned by—issued by—the "government." The term became nearly synonymous with "soldier," and used with great respect.

The use of the term "Angkar" by the Khmers was used in a similar, but far more perverse, manner and traded heavily on the spiritualistic nature of Cambodians. Angkar became a mysterious, unidentified "something" that was all-powerful, all-controlling, to which everybody and everything belonged. A person was no longer an individual, but was the property of Angkar. Not even your very thoughts were your own. If a soldier intended to steal your bike, he would say, "Angkar needs the bike," and that "You will please give it to Angkar." Of course, if you refused, it was not Angkar that shot you, but the soldier asking for it.

Angkar became as feared as the Khmer Rouge. Destruction of a sense of self is accomplished only by application of unending extreme physical and mental pressure. The physical pressure was accomplished with forced slave labor under brutal conditions. Destroying the mind was another thing.

An integral part of the dehumanization of the captives, of the effort to turn them into the property of "Angkar," was non-stop propaganda—or brainwashing, as it has become better known. That mind control process was relentless, eventually robbing the individual of his very personality. Every night, after a sunrise-to-sunset time of hard physical labor, after being fed paltry rations of watery rice, then there were "the meetings."

Captives would be gathered together within the camp. Then, an appointed member of the Khmer Rouge would begin yammering at them with canned propaganda statements aimed at convincing them of how marvelous life was, now that they belonged to Angkar. Of course, any apparent lack of enthusiasm for the message meant that you were not a believer and therefore had to be killed, so there was always one hundred percent participation.

"The thing that I most hated...it frightens me to this day," Albert said about the propagandizing, "is when I hear the word 'meeting.' Call for the meeting. It just kills me. I hate it. It scares me to death. And that's what the Communists did, every night. Every night! They didn't want us to go to sleep. They would say, 'Call for the meeting.' They would call us out, monsoon rain, whatever, they call us out. And then they begin to just wash our brains with this Communist theology, Communist theory. And then they would scream at us, 'Well, did you have enough food today?' and we had to pump our fists in the air and say 'Yes!' But we had nothing. Then they would say, 'Was that food good, today?' We would all yell, 'Yes!' It was just watery rice. That's what they did, all the time."

Even at night, in what would be presumed to be the privacy of the huts while sleeping, one could not be a person. There was no such thing as privacy. Every moment was monitored.

"Every night, they would crawl under our huts, to listen, to see if we talked to each other," Albert said, at one point.

The process gradually shut down rational thought, which of course was the intent. Without rational thought, you were no longer a person. Your thoughts did not belong to you. They belonged to Angkar.

Slave labor has been an unfortunate part of the human story for virtually all of history. The story of the slavery of the Israelites in Egypt is pivotal in the Old Testament. Slavery in America led to the near national suicide of the Civil War. But even as slaves, they were still people, and had value if for no other reason than that their labor was a valued resource. Because of that, they were at least appropriately clothed and treated to, at a minimum, subsistence rations. Not so by the Khmer Rouge.

"I wore the very clothes that I wore when I escaped," Albert said. "The very clothes. Never did we get to change. And even though we grew lots of rice, they never fed us enough. They shipped it all. The way I knew this, one night in our camp, all night long, there were military trucks. I heard them driving. Hundreds of trucks. I found out later they shipped all the rice back to China. And we were starving."

One of the more incomprehensible decisions made early on by Pol Pot and his cadre of leaders—although it was consistent with the image of turning Cambodia into a purely agrarian nation—was to do away with currency. Under the Khmer Rouge, there was no national currency for the exchange of goods. Communist China had supplied the arms and military support for the Khmer Rouge, and they had to be paid. So Pol Pot paid in the only currency he had: rice and fish. Thousands of tons of rice and fish were shipped to China, while the Cambodians who had raised it slowly starved to death.

In an attempt—misguided as were all the policies of Pol Pot—to deal with the problem of feeding millions of slave laborers while shipping all the food to China, a decision was made to force an increase in per-acre rice production. The decree came down that every acre of rice was to produce a minimum of three thousand pounds. Of course, there were no means of achieving this imposed goal. The workers were already being pushed beyond the point of starvation and death. There was no commercial fertilizer, no means of increasing acreage. Of course, the goal was never met, and the workers continued to die of starvation.

"They once sent me to Tonle Sap, to catch fish. Tonle Sap has tons and tons of fish. I caught all kinds of fish; talk about tons of dried fish. And yet, the people...we were not able to eat the fish. They sent it all to China."

Pictures that came to light after World War II of Jewish prisoners in the concentration camps of Germany showed people who looked more like skeletons than humans. They were to be exterminated, so why should food be wasted on them? The same fate was imposed on the captives of the Khmer Rouge, with the added punishment of having to perform slave labor while starving to death.

"I didn't have any weight," Albert replied, laughing. "My ribs all showed. If I wanted to, I could put my finger right between my ribs. If I looked down, I was afraid my eye could drop out, and I'd have to push it back in. If the wind blew strong enough, it would toss my body into the rice field.

"If I would get stuck in the mud, in the rice field, I didn't have strength to get out. If I stayed stuck too long, I'd die right there, in the field. And guess what the Khmer Rouge said? They would tell us, 'That's okay. You'll make good fertilizer.'

"They would tell us, 'If we lose you, we don't lose anything. If you die, we don't have to feed you, and you are good for the rice field.' They don't care if we live or die. It is all the same."

Another common characteristic of the Khmer Rouge was torture. For reasons that are probably outside the realm of understanding on the part of the Western mind, the Khmer Rouge—and they were not alone in this, as the practice was all too common in all of Southeast Asia, at least at that time—seemed to virtually enjoy torturing their captives. One doesn't have to dig very deeply into the sources available on the Khmer Rouge to uncover tales of indescribable practices.

"We were tortured, sometimes," Albert acknowledged. "But at this point, who has the mindset of fearing getting killed? So many times, I begged them, 'Go ahead, and take my life.' When you live with so much death, I don't feel a difference. Living, dying, it doesn't make sense to me.

"Some people committed suicide. In the prisons, the Khmer Rouge put barbed wire around the building, all the way to the top, so they couldn't jump off. People sometimes just gave up, they couldn't stand the torture, the starving. Sometimes they just fell down in the rice paddy, and didn't get up."

A story that is common to anyone surviving the Killing Fields is the story of temptation, of being tempted to eat any living thing that might be surreptitiously caught and slipped into one's mouth. But that tiny frog, that crab that you caught and slipped into your pocket as you planted rice, did not belong to you. It belonged to Angkar. It was your duty to turn it over to a guard. Or else.

"To the Khmer Rouge, there is nothing personal. Everything belongs to the Communists, to 'Angkar.' I remember, one time I saw a little crab crawling along. Nothing belonged to me. Even though I see the crab, it does not belong to me. It belongs to Angkar. What I was supposed to do was catch it and give it to the Khmer Rouge. Instead, I grab it, turn around and put it in my mouth. 'Booosh!' Right there, they beat me, and then dragged me to the village and gave me this whole night of lessons, of Communism.

"They completely brainwash. In another village, a son joined the Khmer Rouge and his father was with the Freedom Fighters.

When the battle came to the village, the Khmer Rouge captured his father. That night at the meeting, villagers try to tell him, 'That is your own father.' He said, 'He is not my father. He is my enemy.' You see, that is how they brainwash. Then, he executed his own father, in front of everybody.

"You just stand there, and watch. The Khmer Rouge watch you. If anybody shows the tear, if they cry, then they beat him, too. They say, 'Why do you have this kind of sympathy? He is the enemy. You cry for the enemy? You must be the enemy, too.' But even if we starve, we still have to work.

"At one point, in the jungle there was this log, a huge log. We have to carry the logs. They wanted me to go ahead and lift up that huge log. I wanted to impress them that I can do this, to favor them. When I try to move the log, I heard this thing in my back just pop. From that time on, my back was never the same. I have trouble with it to this day, and my chest is in great pain.

"There is one other thing I want to tell you," Albert added. "Because there was no medicine, one of the farmers told us about the old Cambodian medicine. There are giant red ants that live in leaves in the jungle. You put these red ants in the urine of a virgin and drink it. So he brings me the urine from his daughter, and I mix it together and I drink it, for the pain. I just squeeze my nose, and I drink it."

Did it work?

"Yeah," he replied, sounding less than convinced. "I drank it because there is too much pain." He was quiet a moment, then laughed as he added an after-thought. "But that horrible smell. I think it gave me even more pain."

Another tactic used for mind control, for assuring that there could be no conspiracies developing among the captives, was to divide and conquer, never giving people a chance to get to know and trust each other.

"We hardly saw each other. That's a tactic they have, moving us, moving us all over. They don't want us to have any way to communicate, to do anything against them. They don't want us to have anything. They would not let us carry anything sharp. That's what people don't understand. They would say, 'Why don't you get up, and fight against them?' For one thing, I don't have the strength. When I tried to move my arms, to try to punch, I can't control my hand. It might swing to the other side. I don't know where it will go. I can't focus. If I stand up, the best thing I can do is try to hold myself in the one spot."

And, of course, there was no way of knowing the fate of any family member. Much of that was by design, to split the family. But to no small degree it was simply a result of the chaotic circumstances, and the isolation of each camp and captive. The attempts to control the mind, as well as the behavior, were very successful. The mind simply shut down, for most captives. And why not? Rational thought would in all probability lead to insanity.

"The only knowledge I had, the only thing I thought about, was 'If I could just have a full spoon of rice.' I didn't have any conscious thought in my brain," Albert acknowledged, "because I didn't have the potential to think anything. My brain was completely washed.

"I still remember at one point, I saw this beautiful, huge white crane flying across the rice field, I struggled hard to keep from weeping. We weren't supposed to cry, but I could barely control it. I kept thinking, if I could just have those wings, and I could fly. At first, it made me angry, that the crane had freedom, could fly away. But seeing that crane was a brief moment of hope."

Hope was not a part of the life of a captive of the Khmer Rouge. It was, instead, a commodity scarce as the rice they grew but were not allowed to eat. It seemed, at times, that the Khmer Rouge soldiers just toyed with the captives, in some diabolical game. Perhaps part of what they did was a form of psychological torment for the sole purpose of destroying hope. Albert related an experience that appears to have been somewhat common.

"I remember one time," he told us, "they took me and tied my arms behind me. The leader took me off and told me he was going to kill me. I knew this was the end. I am dead. But then, he took the ropes off and turned me loose. I don't know why."

That outcome was not the usual case. People were routinely executed for no obvious reason, but sometimes spared for reasons just as obscure. It was a form of irrationality that seems to have no explanation.

"Of course, sometimes I got so starved, so tired, I wanted them to kill me," he added a bit later. "I begged them, 'Cut off my head. Get it over with.' But I stayed alive."

Underlying such depraved treatment of one's fellow man was the simple question of pragmatism, of utility. Why were the Khmer Rouge so bent on killing the very workers they needed? What was behind all the brutality, and using people until they died?

"I think it involved so much the hatred," Albert said, attempting an answer to that question. "The hatred between the Khmer Rouge and the Freedom Fighters (government forces), the hate during the war with the bombing, the killing, and the hate about the culture class, the different cultures. They knew that in order to keep the people under control, it would be so hard to control the people who are educated, instead of completely dumb. The peasant people, people they call part of the Revolution, they wanted to keep. People like us...they wanted to get rid of us."

At one point, the Khmer Rouge leaders realized, they were basically running out of people. Rice doesn't harvest itself, and the Khmer Rouge weren't about to do the work. They needed replacements, so used equally brutal tactics of population replacement. Young men and women were forced to "marry" and produce more babies. The babies, of course, became property of Angkar. The leaders knew if they had the children from birth, they could be raised to be faithful followers of the Revolution. They would become part of the new Kampuchea.

"They had a special place for the babies, because they knew that was how they control. When a mother had a baby, it was taken away, and the mother forced to work in the fields," Albert added.

For more than three years, life and time ceased to have meaning for Albert, and the many others like him. Each day was the same as the day before and the day after. For most of us, there is a sense of time passing. We look forward to holidays, to vacations, we anticipate the changing of seasons. Our families grow, goals are achieved, or perhaps we fall short. But always, there is yesterday, and tomorrow. Next month is Christmas, next year we graduate from college. Time passes, but as it does it has meaning and context.

Not so for the wretched victims suffering under the inhumane treatment of the Khmer Rouge. Tomorrow meant nothing. Today meant nothing. You were alive, but that meant nothing. Even in battle, when life and death are separated only by the fickle irony of fate, at least there is hope—hope for survival, hope that the battle will be won, hope that the war will eventually end. One can hope that someday it will all be over, and you can go home.

But for Albert, and all those with him, there was no such basis for hope. For those unfortunate beings, deprived of all the basic essentials of life and humanity, there was no discernible basis for hope. And certainly, there were no rational reasons to believe that life would ever change, but would only someday end. And there was no home to go to.

Chapter 6

Freedom

...the sound of a driven leaf shall put them to flight, and they shall flee as one flees from the sword, and they shall fall though no one pursues.

Leviticus 26:36

Hope is an elusive condition, in the human experience. Erik Erickson, the psychoanalyst famous for coining the phrase "identity crisis," once said about hope,

> "Hope is both the earliest and the most indispensable virtue inherent in the state of being alive. If life is to be sustained hope must remain, even where confidence is wounded, trust impaired."

Compare that thought, however, with the following assertion by Friedrich Nietzsche, the nineteenth-century German philosopher,

> "Hope is the worst of evils, for it prolongs the torments of man."

Where "confidence is wounded, trust impaired," as Erickson said, hope is all that may keep us alive, or give us reason to want to stay alive. Hope springs eternal, someone once said. Yet, when there is no discernible, or credible, basis for having hope, to remain hopeful can be a cruel thing. As Nietzsche said, it "prolongs the torments of man," and in that sense could even be considered cruel.

And that was life under the Khmer Rouge, the life experienced by Albert and those who shared his fate. They had nothing to go on, but hope. But hope in what, hope for what? They were living in the most cruel of conditions, in total isolation—both from those around them as well as from the outside world. They had no way of knowing if anyone knew, or cared, about their condition, or that they even existed. They had no reason of any sort to believe that some "cavalry" was over the horizon, about to ride in and rescue them. To hope for any form of salvation, when there was no reason to believe salvation would ever be forthcoming, would have, as Nietzsche said, prolonged the torment.

But we are created for life, and hope is part of life. Although Albert and the others had no way of knowing it, there was, in fact, reason for hope. Things were not going well for Pol Pot and his Khmer Rouge. His experiment in the transformation of Cambodia into an agrarian utopia was steadily coming unraveled. He had long since killed off all those who could have helped sustain and operate his country, and was systematically killing off a goodly portion of the worker bees who were essential to feeding the country. Adding to those woes, there was dissension developing within his own regime. Ho Chi Minh and his North Vietnamese leaders sensed this growing weakness and began planning an invasion.

Pol Pot turned to his ally, China, who promised him the support of supplies, but the fighting would be up to him. Given the weakened condition of Cambodia, and the strength that Ho Chi

Minh's forces had gained with the defeat of the Americans in Vietnam, the outcome of any invasion by Vietnam was preordained. On Christmas Day of 1978, the invasion began. Vietnamese forces quickly began overrunning Khmer Rouge positions in eastern Cambodia, and it was not long before Phnom Penh was threatened. It was only a matter of time—very little time as it turned out—before the regime of the infamous son of Cambodia, Pol Pot, was crumbling across the country.

And at what point did things change for Albert? When did he begin to be aware that something was happening, as the Vietnamese forces closed in, driving the Khmer Rouge out?

"After 1975, when the Khmer Rouge took over," Albert replied, "through 1977, we hardly ever heard even a gunshot. If they wanted to kill somebody, they just smashed their heads in, or killed them in horrible ways. They were not worth even wasting a bullet. Then in 1978, I began to hear guns again, and it began getting closer and closer. I think, *Oh. It must be the battles are beginning again. It must be another war.* And then I began to see the military helicopters, that we haven't seen in a long time. Then, it was the same bazookas and rockets I heard in Phnom Penh, right in front of me."

Vietnamese forces steadily, and quickly, pushed their way across Cambodia from the east, driving the rag-tag Khmer Rouge soldiers ahead of them, overrunning the camps. As each camp fell, and was left undefended, the captives were on their own. For Albert, it meant the end to nearly four years of darkness and evil. As the Vietnamese encountered the soldiers at his camp, a battle broke out.

"I was at a camp near Battambang. And the Khmer Rouge there, they couldn't handle the battle. They were being killed. They soon began to panic and run. And when they ran off, there was no one guarding us. And that is how I escaped."

Albert had said that there were fifteen who had managed to gain each other's trust, and escaped together. The question came up as to how that had been possible, when the captives were never allowed to talk to each other, even at night when the soldiers might be eavesdropping under where you were sleeping.

"We saw each other daily," Albert explained, "and even though we may not talk, we would look at each other, we could see in the eye. You know in your heart that he is trying to tell you something. You can see the evil in the eye of an evil person, the soldier, and you can see the eye that is soft, that has trust. They are completely different."

After living for years in abject fear, unable to even think, how do you suddenly decide that it is safe to make a break for it? How does the mind suddenly start functioning again, become rational again, allowing you to decide to run?

"I could see the battle going on," Albert said. "It was two hundred, maybe three hundred yards away. The Vietnamese were attacking, and the Khmer Rouge, they were at the point of death. They ran off, running for their lives, and left us. We realized this was our chance, so we just grabbed each other and took off running. And that is how we escaped into the jungle.

"I don't know, at that point, where the strength came from...I don't know where. It just came from...for so long, freedom was...it was all gone. We couldn't even think about it. Now we could run, and we didn't even think about anything but running.

"The others didn't know where to go. They came to me to lead them," Albert continued. "Everyone in the camp was in a panic, and scattered. Everyone just ran for their lives, in all directions."

The situation was most likely quite chaotic, with gunfire, people running in every which direction, yelling and screaming. In retrospect, it was impressive that the fifteen had sufficient presence of mind—given they had virtually lost the capacity for thought, by then—to organize even to that extent. There was no doubt in Albert's mind where he would lead his little flock.

"Oh, yes. I headed west. You remember, that was my first plan, when I left Phnom Penh. We headed west, for Thailand."

Heading west was a good idea, and proved to be a lifesaver for Albert. But heading west, while in dense jungle, with no compass, is easier said than done. Albert relied on his many trips with Uncle Hank to lead him on.

"Mostly, we relied on the sun. Sun rises in the east, sets in the west. At night, we had the moon, the stars, if we could see them. Sometimes, the jungle was too dense to see anything, or it was overcast. I would hug a big tree and try to sense the side that was warmer from the sun. I knew it would be on the south side of the tree, so I would be facing north and my left arm would be west. I knew that as long as I keep going west, I am going toward a free country—Thailand."

Free at last from years of horrific treatment, the group ran first on fear and adrenalin. Then, as energy and strength quickly drained from bodies that had none to spare, they had to settle down and begin to pace themselves. Although they were free from the camp and immediate captivity, they were not out of danger. In a very real sense they were moving from the frying pan into the fire, as they worked their way westward toward the border, and had to be especially careful.

"Along the border it was just chaos," Albert said. "Some of the Khmer Rouge scattered, running for their lives from the North Vietnamese attacks. There were old guerrilla groups still in the jungle and there were Thai soldiers there. And there were always bandits in the jungle. It was a very dangerous place. We traveled mostly at night, so we wouldn't get caught. If we got caught, we were dead."

It is approximately seventy-five miles as the crow flies from Battambang, west to the Thai border. Much of the jungle in that area was pretty heavy going, with tall, thick grass and lots of brush. It's hard to imagine the group making more than two or three miles a night, with little idea of where they were or whether they were making any progress.

"Yes, the jungle is very dense," Albert agreed. "We had to just push through the heavy undergrowth. I was a good climber. Sometimes I climbed up to the tree tops, to see where we were going. But most of the time, we just headed west. We knew that someday, we would get to Thailand—if we didn't get caught."

It's hard for those of us who have never trekked through a jungle barefooted to imagine doing so, under any conditions. But couple that with the fact that they were already on the verge of starvation and it begins to seem beyond belief. And once again, as always, there was the issue of food. What do you eat while making your way through the underbrush of a jungle?

"Oh, we ate anything we could get our hands on. Rats, whatever. We ran into a lot of cobras. We mostly ate cobras," he said, rather matter-of-factly.

Eating snakes isn't unknown—rattlesnake steaks are featured at the annual Rattlesnake Roundup in the United States. All that notwithstanding, making them your normal daily fare is an entirely different issue. There were two immediate issues with doing that. First, and perhaps foremost, is that your daily entrée is quite poisonous.

"Oh, yeah," Albert confirmed, "cobras are very poisonous. One strike, you're dead."

The second issue is, how do you go about transforming the cobra from being a live snake crawling through the brush to being the evening meal? That is, how do you kill a cobra bare-handed, without getting killed by them?

"With sticks. I killed them with sticks," he explained, making it sound too easy. "Actually, I used two sticks. I sort of poked at the cobra with one stick, to make it raise up, puff up its head. You wave the stick in front of its eyes, to distract it. Then, just at the right moment, I hit it on the head and knocked it to the ground. I had another stick with a fork on the end, and I quickly pinned down its head to the ground. Then I killed it with the other stick."

But that wasn't the end of the story. As with most things, there's a right way and a wrong way.

"Some people were very afraid of the cobra, and used a long stick. That is how they got killed by the cobra. They can't hit the head fast enough, or they miss. Then the cobra got itself wrapped around the stick, and when they jerked the stick back up the cobra would fall down on them and strike them. You have to use a shorter stick."

Once the snake was dead, Albert had an advantage that may seem a minor thing, on face value, but one that was invaluable to the group's well being—he had a makeshift knife to use to skin and cut up the snake. And how does one who would have been tortured, and probably killed, by the Khmer Rouge for having such a weapon come by a knife?

"As we were escaping the camp," Albert explained, "we passed where the blacksmith worked. There was the blade of a knife he had been making, so I stole it. There was no handle, but I made one from bamboo. Having that knife was a big help to us, in the jungle."

Once the cobra, or any other form of meat, was dead, skinned and cut up, did they have to eat it raw or was it possible to cook it? If so, how? They certainly would not have had a supply of matches.

"Oh no, we cooked them. There is a plant in Cambodia that has a soft inside, sort of like the cattail. We pulled it out and carried it in a bamboo stick, to use to start a fire. We have the rock—what do you call it, flint rock?—for starting the fire, and just strike it. We would make a spark from flint rock to start the dry tinder we carried with us."

Of course, there was always a concern about a fire being seen by the Khmer Rouge, or the other threatening groups in the area. Having a fire could have been dangerous.

"Yes," Albert agreed. "We had to cook in the daytime, and travel at night. We didn't make a big fire, just a little one to cook on."

Their escape attempt took place during the dry period. While that made it far easier to travel through the jungle, finding water to drink became a real problem. Most of the time they collected sap off tree leaves and vines. But even that had its problems.

"One time, I used the wrong leaves. They were poisonous, like poison ivy or poison oak. I got blisters all over my lips and mouth," he said, laughing at himself.

While Albert related his experiences, one could only wonder what it would have been like, buried in dense jungle, struggling along unmeasured distances to an unknown, unseen destination. How does a person in that environment keep a sense of purpose, of progress, or have any sense of where you are, day by day? How could you keep from wondering if you were just wandering in random paths in the jungle? In truth, the group had little sense of where they were or if they were making progress.

There was an aspect of the ordeal of getting through the jungle that wouldn't be apparent to those who have lived their lives in freedom. For Albert and his group it was, in fundamental ways, an improvement in their lives.

"No, we didn't really know where we were," Albert confirmed. "At one point, I saw Sisophon (a town in far northwest Cambodia, between Battambang and the Thai border) in the distance. I knew we were closer. But at least I enjoyed every moment that I was free. No one was beating me, or doing any of the horrible things they did to me. Even though I was in the depths of the jungle, and could be struck by the cobra at any moment...I enjoyed it."

Albert was trained in ways of the jungle by his Uncle Hank, so was reasonably capable of knowing how to take care of himself, and survive. But what about the others? How did they take all the hardship of getting through the jungle? How did they know what to do?

"Oh, they mostly looked to me," Albert said, "they did what I did. But the Khmer Rouge, they had made them used to hardship, so they could do it. We were all like a machine, by then, we just did what we had to do."

Those comments said unspoken volumes about what they had all suffered. It is virtually impossible for most people to comprehend that struggling barefooted through dense jungles, living on cobras and rats, drinking sap from vines that could be poisonous, could in a sense seem like an improvement in your life and standard of living. Then, too, there was always the threat of the Khmer Rouge patrols, and the other armed groups roaming around the jungle. Albert had originally been captured by simply stumbling onto such a patrol and finding himself surrounded. What was to keep that from happening again?

Albert answered that question with a simple demonstration. He got out of his rocking chair, went to a coffee table and picked up a small glass jar filled with serving spoons and forks. He rattled the spoons around, listening to them clink on the glass, at the pace of a person walking.

"I know that sound to this very day," he said, sitting back down. "They were everywhere. We ran into them, several times. I was so used to the sound of them. They carried the AK-47s, and I knew the sound it made when they carried it. And the other stuff they carried, the ammunition and water cans, all made a jingle sound. We would hear them coming, and just bury ourselves in the jungle, till they were past.

"We ran into them several times. I remember, one time they came so close. So close. We just pressed flat against the ground, so flat we could hardly breathe. I thought, *This is it.* But they didn't see us."

Finding something to eat—even rats or cobras—was a constant struggle. The group had subsisted on a near-starvation diet for all the time they were in captivity, so they were accustomed to having little—and sometimes nothing—to eat. But that also meant their bodies were already malnourished.

"No, no such luck," Albert said, a bit ruefully, about whether they were able to find food every day. "But that just shows the miracle of God. Our bodies are a miracle of God, the way it can survive without food and still keep going. People who don't believe in God's miracles don't even look at their own bodies. There is the miracle, right there, and how wonderful it is. How it can survive. And I don't even have to tell it to keep on breathing. Even when I don't care if I live, or not, it just keeps on breathing whether I tell it to, or not. That is so wonderful, the way God does that."

There is no way of knowing, no archive of records to research to determine how long Albert and his friends were in the jungle. It must have been weeks, and perhaps months. But finally, one fateful night, they saw a light gleaming through the thicket of trees, brush and vines. They had made it to the border of Thailand, to freedom. If—they could get to that light.

Few of us have a basis, a context, for comprehending what Albert must have felt the first moment he saw that light. There are moments in our lives that are memorable, our "Kodak" moments, but what could compare to that moment for Albert? There are the pictures burned in our history of prisoners of war coming out of the prison camps to freedom. But few of us ever personally experience such a dramatic event. What would go through a person's mind at such a time, when you finally see the light that means you have survived the worst that could be done to you, that you are about to become a free person, again?

Albert had to reflect for a few moments, before he was able to comment on his thoughts and feelings at that time. Perhaps he was trying to remember an event that was, by now, decades in the past. Perhaps it was too emotional, too meaningful to be able to easily describe. But after hesitating, he tried to explain his feelings.

"For so many months, it was just pitch black. We seldom could see anything. I saw thousands of lightning bugs, and we would sometimes see the full moon and stars, but never anything else. Even in the daytime, it was dark in the jungle. Then one night I saw this incredible light, just incredible. Then in my mind I thought, *Oh, it must be some kind of city. It might be Thailand.* Later on, it turned out to be the United Nations camp. They put the lights all around. It was the first time that I saw the light. It was hard to believe that it was real. I wanted to jump, and celebrate. When I saw that light…no matter what, I don't want to lose that light. I will cut through anything at all. I want to go to that light."

Of course, the ordeal was anything but over. Between Albert and his group, and that distant light, was a jungle far more deadly than the cobras he had faced. And that raised a serious issue. Both sides had mined the border in many places, for many years. But how could they know what lay in front of them, for good or ill? Did they have any way of knowing the area was mined?

"This is how I knew," he answered, with a shrug that seemed to suggest a feeling of 'What were we supposed to do, just stand there?' Then he answered the question. "One of us stepped on a mine, and it blew him to pieces. Then the mortars began, and all of a sudden, blam, blam, blam, blam, the machine guns opened fire. We just kept on running, kept on running, toward the light."

It was known that Albert and his friends had to run that gantlet of mines, small arms fire and mortars as they made their last desperate dash for freedom. But knowing that didn't answer why. What could possibly have justified that? Who was shooting at them? Why were they shooting at them?

"The history of Thai and Cambodians," Albert explained, "is they hate each other. They don't want Cambodians coming over. And too, there were Khmer Rouge patrols in the area. I heard Khmer voices, sometimes. And there were the guerrillas, the Freedom Fighters who buried themselves in the jungle to escape the Khmer Rouge. There was lots of tension, along the border. The Thai soldiers took no chances. They just started shooting at anything. But I just kept on running, running to the light.

"The field wasn't really open. There were lots of big trees, small trees and bushes. I fell sometimes, stumbled over a bush or log. I would just get up, keep on running."

All fifteen of the group had survived the trek through the jungle, had made it through to see the lights of the camp. They were still all together when they started to run. Then, one of them stepped on a mine, and alerted the Thai troops—and that's when the firing started. By then, Albert knew he had no choice but to keep running. Turning back was not an option, and standing still meant certain death.

"I heard the AK-47s, the M-16s, the different sounds, and saw the tracers (incendiary bullets used so that the one firing could see where the bullets were going) all around me, like lightning bugs, just everywhere.

"I was just running for my life. All I could think is, *They are after me again.* It was more painful, more frightening to get captured again, so I didn't care if I got hit by a bullet."

At some point—he doesn't remember exactly when, in all the noise and chaos, and his mind was incapable of rational thought at the time, anyway—the vision of the white crane came back to him.

"One time when I was working in the rice fields, when life was so full of evil and so horrible," Albert remembered, "I looked up and saw a large, white crane flying over me. I wanted to cry, but of course I couldn't let the Khmer Rouge see me crying. It seemed so unfair that the crane could fly free, and I was trapped, and so lost. But at some point, while I was trying to get through the mines and the bullets, I remember that I thought, *If I can get through this, I will be free. But if I die, at least I will die free.*"

Mankind has been willing to put life on the line, to die, to obtain freedom, throughout all history. Obviously, Albert and his friends were willing to pay that price. The bright light of freedom represented by the distant lights of the UN camp drew them onward, through the brush and trees, through the bombs and bullets.

"It was a hundred yards—maybe two hundred yards, I don't really know how far it was—that I ran through all that. When I finally got across, I fell down. Then I saw a truck, with the big red cross on the side, coming to me. Some men jumped out and grabbed me, picked me up. They knew that the Thai soldiers would look for me. If they found me, they would kill me.

"After I was taken into the camp, and got my number, later I could look across where I came. I looked across the field, and thought about that night, I just broke down and wept. I thought, *How did I make it across?* I don't know. I don't remember."

Albert didn't learn for some time that only he, and one other of the group of fifteen, had survived.

"I heard the mines blowing up, heard the screaming. I had no mind for knowing what was happening, and I knew I couldn't help if I stopped. I just threw my body through the bushes, kept on going."

And don't forget—he was barefoot.

"Oh my, you should have seen my foot, the calluses. They were thick, like that," he said, laughing, holding his finger and thumb an inch apart. "Even if I stepped on a thorn, I wouldn't feel it. My whole body was just cut and torn. All the old pain, all of it was there after I got through.

"The Thai soldiers were in position along the border. When I got past them, running to the camp, it was a moment of chaos for me…I couldn't take it. I couldn't understand it. It was the kind of life that whatever happens, just happens. I couldn't think of anything when I saw the truck, with the big red cross on the side. It had come to me, to get me. They helped me in. I couldn't understand the language.

"I came all the way out of the jungle to hear this strange language—the first time in my life I hear the English," he mentioned, smiling at the memory of it.

Incongruous as it might have been, there was one other enduring memory from that night, of being picked up by the truck with the red cross on it, that offered a clue to yet another facet of Albert's personality—he has a wry sense of humor.

"I really enjoyed the ride," he said, laughing at the memory. "All I could think, it was my first time to ride in a truck. I really enjoyed the truck ride."

After nearly four years of indescribable horror, of hideous treatment, constant exposure to violent and brutal death and the threat of death, of hoping and pleading for death, Cheng Sophanarith—the name given him by his mother, a name that she had learned from the Venable at the Temple meant power, or potential—had survived.

He later learned that his mother and father had both been executed. As another example of the insanity of the Khmer Rouge, the eldest child of the Cheng family, Albert's sister Phana who had been a nurse in Pursat Province, had also been brutally murdered. Her husband, who had been a medical technician, had also been executed. What regime ever killed off the very people needed to care for the living? His brother, Chawvy, and sister, Srey, had also been killed. Much of his family had been destroyed.

Ten years would have to pass before he began to feel human again, and the nightmares of his life begin to fade. But for now—he was alive, and safe within the confines of a United Nations camp somewhere in Thailand. His second life was about to start, and his "potential" discovered.

Albert didn't know, and it could never be definitively established, the name or location of the camp where he had arrived. Tracing his records was next to impossible by virtue of the fact he could no longer remember the assumed name he was using at the time he came to the camp, or when he resumed use of his family name.

The United Nations installed and operated a number of refugee camps in Thailand as refugees streamed into the country to escape the Khmer Rouge, a stream that turned into a flood as the Khmer Rouge were overrun by the invading armies of Vietnam. Maps of such camp locations showed most of the camps either along the northern border of Cambodia—far from the direction that Albert headed—or more to the southwest, west of Pursat Province. Those maps did not indicate any camps directly west of Battambang. One possibility was a camp to the northwest, along a line that passed close to the town of Sisophon, which he had seen while enroute through the jungle.

In truth, it hardly matters, other than to satisfy the curiosity of a researcher, exactly when it was he arrived there, or which camp it may have been. What matters is that Albert survived to make it to that camp, that he survived to start a new life. Knowing more of those details would have been interesting, perhaps, but would have added little to his story. There was another issue of greater importance, and that was the question of Albert's spiritual journey during his captivity. Did he appeal to Buddha to protect him, or did he feel abandoned, that there was no God?

He didn't have to think about his answer.

"Chaos," he quickly responded. "I was just completely lost. It was the Khmer Rouge, they were a big threat to me, constantly. It was just breathe in, breathe out. It was just the Khmer Rouge, not anything else. From my experience in the jungle (before captivity) I knew there is something, a supernatural power, someplace. In our culture, we have many idols, many gods. We believe our ancestors are part of that supernatural force. When I would pray, I prayed for my ancestors, too.

"Sometimes, I asked 'Is there a God? Where is God?' I could see the material gods of my culture—things like stones, statues of the Buddha, and bones of dead relatives—but I felt there was something more, beyond what I could see. I always had the feeling that I was seeking something that I couldn't find. But most of the time…my mind was just blank. I had no thought at all, except to do what I am told, don't make the Khmer Rouge mad, don't get beaten or tortured."

William Ernest Henley lay suffering in a hospital bed when he wrote his famous poem, *"Invictus,"* Latin for "invincible." That poem begins with the lines:

> *Out of the night that covers me,*
> *Black as the Pit from pole to pole…*

and ends with the lines:

> *I am the master of my fate:*
> *I am the captain of my soul.*

Henley is to be admired for the courage he demonstrated in his own life, and for the sentiment that the poem conjures. But Henley was not a captive of the Khmer Rouge. It is difficult to imagine that Albert Cheng ever felt "invincible" during his four years in the black pit that covered his soul, or that he ever felt that he was "the master of his fate, the captain of his soul."

Numerous heroic stories have been told of prisoners, from the Apostle Paul in the chains of the Roman Emperor, soon to be martyred, to pilots shot down over North Vietnam who survived years of pain and torture at the hands of their captors by relying on the mighty fortress that is our God. Like Albert, they were not the masters of their fate. Unlike Albert, they could be the captains of their souls. Paul had faith in his Savior, Jesus Christ, and knew that his life would not end with his death.

The war prisoners knew that they had a country and government seeking their release, and many of them had the strength of their Christian faith. They had that source of hope and strength for which Albert had been seeking all his life, but had yet to find. As the Khmer Rouge progressively destroyed both his body and his soul, all Albert could do was ask, "Where is God?"

Albert's spiritual journey, seeking that "something" that his heart and soul longed for, obviously did not end with his escape. Indeed, it had just begun. But it would require flying to a strange new country half-way round the world, before the journey would end and the seeker be found. Getting to take that trip to the strange new world would not happen for nearly two more years. But for now, Albert was safe. And for the moment, that was all that mattered.

Section IV
Finding The Light

Chapter 7

Coming to America

And after you have suffered a little while, the God of all grace, who has called you to his eternal glory in Christ, will himself restore, establish, and strengthen you.

1 Peter 5:10

The closing scene in the 1957 movie *The Bridge On The River Kwai* is unforgettable. In the story, a group of British soldiers has been captured by the Japanese, and forced to assist in building a bridge over the River Kwai as part of a railroad to be used for hauling supplies to the Japanese Army. The bridge becomes a moral conflict. Obviously, it will aid the enemy. But to help build it is also a means of keeping the soldiers occupied, their minds off their dire circumstances. The British superior officer believes the benefit to his men is worth the conflict, and orders his men to put their all into building it. But in the end, the bridge cannot be permitted to stand. British Commandos are secretly sent in to destroy it.

At the end of the movie, a British medic who had been part of the group stands viewing the resultant carnage. The British superior officer is dead, the Commandos are dead, the Japanese head of the prison camp has committed suicide, the bridge and the first train that attempted to cross it lie in smoldering ruins in the river. The medic looks at it all, and says the memorable closing line:

"Madness! Madness!"

There seems to be no more fitting assessment of the four years of the Khmer Rouge, of the four years that Albert suffered at their hands. It was madness. No other word seems to fit. Finally, though, for Albert Cheng the nightmare seemed to be over, the madness ended. Unfortunately, his nightmares wouldn't end for years to come.

"It took me ten years, at least, before all the frightening memories, the nightmares, began to go away," he commented about the time.

But at least he was now safe. He was logged into the UNBRO camp under the last name he had assumed—for the simple reason he could no longer remember his real name—his picture was taken and he was given an ID badge to wear so he could get his ration of rice and fish. The rations weren't overly large, but they were the first real meals he had eaten in nearly four years—and they certainly beat rats and cobras.

Though now safe and better fed, with some freedom within the camp, he was still a prisoner and not allowed to leave the camp. Given the historic bad relations between the two countries, the Thai government was to be commended for allowing the United Nations and other refugee support groups to set up and operate the camps. And as the Khmer Rouge government disintegrated, the refugee tide was becoming a tsunami, threatening to overwhelm all efforts to deal with it. In that respect, it could be understood that the Thai government did everything possible to discourage the influx, and contain those who made it. They most certainly did not want a flood of Cambodians swarming across their country.

"The Thai government, they could get rid of us at any time," Albert confirmed.

In fact, tens of thousands of Cambodians and other refugees were forcibly repatriated to Cambodia by the Thai government before the fall of the Khmer Rouge. Many of those people either died crossing the minefields at the border, or were later executed, or died, at the hands of the Khmer Rouge. Although Albert was still a prisoner, his life was not harsh, with none of the brutality of the Khmer Rouge. He had sufficient food, began to lose his emaciated appearance, and received medical treatment when needed. They even attempted to provide some entertainment, by showing movies.

"When I was in the first camp, they showed us movies, once in a while. Out in the field, they had a big screen, a sheet, and showed us movies. It was the first time I had ever seen a movie. One night, they showed an old Jesus film. I couldn't understand the language. It was this strange language called 'English.' They weren't translating into the Khmer language, at all.

"I couldn't understand what they were talking about. I just watched the people on the screen. I saw this man, I didn't know who he was. But he seemed kind, and did good things for the people. But to my shock he ended up being nailed to the wood. I didn't know the cross, what they called it, then. I couldn't understand why they killed the good man, who did all the good things for the people."

That comment was a surprise, but perhaps shouldn't have been. The story of Jesus, His birth, death on the cross and resurrection are quite familiar to most in the West, even if not Christian. Christmas and Easter are celebrated nationally, if not for religious reasons then at least for marketing reasons. And for those who grew up in a Christian home, and in largely Christian communities, most would never have thought about the fact that the historical Jesus might be completely unknown to a significant number of the world's population.

For the vast majority of Cambodians, Christ and Christianity were absolute unknowns. In his book, *Killing Fields, Living Fields*, Don Cormack traces in great detail the history of the Christian church in Cambodia. Although some inroads were being made during the twentieth century, most Cambodians remained unaware of the strange new religion. When Phnom Penh fell, many of the leaders of the struggling Christian churches, as well as those who professed Christianity, were brutally executed or died in the prison camps. The church was dealt a staggering, but not lethal, blow. A later chapter provides more detail on recent attempts to re-establish the Christian church in Cambodia.

In retrospect, it should not have been surprising that Albert was puzzled by the strange movie. But it did raise a question of how the movie affected Albert while he was watching it. Albert was a good person, a kind person who never harmed anyone. He did good things for his family and for other people. And yet, he was treated brutally, nearly killed, by the Khmer Rouge. Did he think about that, while watching the "good man be nailed to the wood?"

It took a few moments, as he thought about it, before he responded to the question.

"I don't think I could think of anything, like that," he said rather quietly, "because my heart was just too heavy, then. I was missing my family, I had so many frightening things in my mind. At one point, when I saw the white crane flying free, I did have some thoughts about how I wished I could just fly away from these human beings, because I couldn't understand the kind of torture and suffering.

"So, to me at the time, I would sometimes think there just had to be a way I could leave, be away from all the suffering. I would think, *There must be a God, somewhere.* I would think about the old culture, about the ancestors and the Buddha and things. But most of the time, my mind was just a blank. I could think of nothing but doing what I was told."

Albert had been trained as a boy in the Buddhist temple to meditate, and said he often did so out in the jungle with his Uncle Hank. It raised the question of whether he attempted meditation while a captive, to help keep some kind of inner peace—or at least his sanity. Of course, letting them see him do it was out of the question. But even though he knew he couldn't show it, did he attempt it in his mind?

Albert's face brightened at the question.

"Oh, I could just do it anytime. That is part of my nature, something that grew inside of me. I could put myself in tune with the spirit."

Of course, the Khmer Rouge didn't allow any form of worship in any fashion. Doing so openly was a death sentence, and they slaughtered hundreds, perhaps thousands, of professing Christians.

"Oh, no, we couldn't worship. I remember when they came to the temple and just shot the monks, killed all the monks. Blood was everywhere. It was so shocking. But in my heart, I still longed for that...something."

In fact, during the four years of the Khmer Rouge, many thousands of monks were slaughtered, and temples damaged or destroyed. Many stories were told of monks being shot down in front of people, just to show that the Buddha had no power over the Khmer Rouge, that chants, amulets and fetishes couldn't stop bullets from an AK-47.

As days passed in the refugee camp, a certain routine developed and Albert adjusted to his new life. There were teachers at the camp who began helping those who chose to do so learn some basic English. Albert had no idea, at least early on, that he would be coming to America, but attended the English classes to help pass time, if nothing else.

"After a while, I was taken to a different UN camp, deep inside Thai country," he said. "We had a bit more freedom than at the first camp, but we still were watched all the time by Thai police.

"At the second camp, they let us work, and paid us Thai money. They had shops in the camps where we could buy things, buy food. And the Thai people had push carts in the camp, selling things. It was the first time in all the years of darkness under the Communists that I could buy food, get something I wanted."

Americans, by and large, are goal oriented, future oriented. We're always thinking in terms of what we will be doing tomorrow, next week, next year. How, any such person would have to wonder, do you live day after day when you have no concept of knowing what tomorrow holds, far less what your future holds or even what country you might be in at some future point? Yet, that was what the refugees in the UN camps had to contend with, to live with, for months—and for many of them, several years.

Before it all ended, Albert spent approximately two years in the refugee camps. In some respects, those years were just as lost as were the years in captivity. Although not harshly treated, he was still in captivity, with little to do to make a day go faster, or to break the tedium. He remembers little, good or bad, of those times. Yet, they were probably good for him, perhaps even necessary. His mind needed time to heal, even more so than did his body. And the best medicine for his abused mind was time, days of doing little, of having no conflicts, no fear of torture or death, no concern about whether he would have anything to eat. Just quiet, empty, healing time. As beneficial as that time may have been, though, as days passed the time came when the question of his future had to be addressed.

"There was information around the camp," he explained, when asked about how he made the decision to come to America. "We were told that there were sponsors around the world that might sponsor you to come to their country. We had interviews, and had to fill out forms. But I really didn't have a clue. I especially couldn't think of leaving Cambodia. It was so difficult for me. I didn't have a thought about leaving my own country, for another world that I don't even know. But, I knew it would be impossible for me to go back."

Obviously, he couldn't go back to Cambodia with the Khmer Rouge still in power. And with Vietnam taking over, it might have been just as risky. Thailand certainly didn't want the refugees there indefinitely so he would be forced to leave, sooner or later. What his fate might be if no sponsor could be found was a question he was incapable of asking himself, and certainly couldn't answer.

"No, I had no idea, no thoughts," he said, shaking his head. "Besides, at that time, my mind was still in such a state of shock. I was wrapped up with the sorrow, the sadness, the loss, all those things inside of me. I couldn't think."

Nevertheless, the day came that he learned he had a sponsor, that he was going to leave.

"There was a Christian group," Albert recalled. "I don't remember what they were called. They told me they would sponsor me. Then they called me for an interview. I guess I must have done what everybody else did. They have applications, ask you what country you want to go to. I guess I must have filled out one of those."

The sponsoring group was the USCC, the United States Catholic Conference, now known as the US Conference of Catholic Bishops. This group worked closely with the Red Cross and other organizations to find sponsors for Cambodian refugees to come to America. Albert was one of the fortunate ones included in this resettling effort. There were many legal and logistical hurdles to clear before final approval was granted but the time came when he learned he had been accepted, that he was headed for a new life in a strange place called America.

"After I knew for sure I would be leaving, they had a short training for when we were to go to the United States. They showed us how to buckle our seat belts, on the airplane, and what the airplane would be like, and go step by step when we are on the way. I had a fun time with that, too.

"Then the day we were to leave, they came with a bus, the first time I got to see this huge bus. We got our bags, and our tags and papers. Then we walked out of the prison to the bus. We were watched at all times by the Thai soldiers, I guess to make sure we don't run off into the jungle, or something. Then they took us to Bangkok. Can you imagine? Here you come from the jungle— cobras, monkeys, everything—then here you are, in Bangkok! And this huge, huge Boeing. We walked like monkeys to this huge Boeing.

"There were also the other folks, these mountain people from way, way over to the Cambodian border with Laos, that came on the airplane," he added, smiling as he remembered the "mountain people" on the Boeing.

There is no way of knowing for sure, but it is possible that they could have been members of the Montagnards—"mountain people," in French—the indigenous people of the mountainous areas of northeastern Cambodia and Laos. During the Vietnam

War, because the Ho Chi Minh trail went through the area, US forces enlisted the aid of the Montagnards as guides, informants and aides. They were extremely reliable and useful to the US forces.

After the fall of Saigon to North Vietnam, thousands of Montagnards fled to escape reprisals from the Viet Cong. It was quite possible that these were the people who were on the plane with Albert. Many of those people had never been out of their isolated mountain villages, and were now on a Boeing 747 headed for America.

"It was so funny," Albert recalled, laughing. "Every where they go, they carry this bamboo on their back."

The "bamboo," as Albert described it, was a hollow pipe, two to four inches in diameter and perhaps two feet long, slung over their shoulder on a leather thong.

"That is how they smoke their tobacco," he continued. "And their whole body is naked, except for these short pants. They don't know how to wear clothes. And can you imagine, they walk onto this Boeing, like that? During the interview, you tell them you are going to take them to America, or wherever, and they don't care. But you tell them they can't take the bamboo, they say, 'You don't have to take me. I stay.' They won't go without the bamboo. They put water in it, then grind up tobacco, or marijuana, and put in it, then they smoke it. They let out these big clouds of smoke, like a train engine. I have so much fun, laughing at that.

"I remember, they had never seen an automatic door. When we walked into the airport—I think it was in San Francisco—they come to this door and all of a sudden it just opens up, like magic. They all jump back, and run off. And when they see a mirror, and see themselves, they go around to the back to see who is on the other side. I thought that was so funny."

Those of us of a certain age remember reading Mark Twain's *A Connecticut Yankee In King Arthur's Court*, the story of a nineteenth-century American who by some strange phenomenon gets transported back to the days of the Knights of the Round Table. The story is a series of comparisons of the strange conflicts that would naturally arise between "modern" and ancient cultures. That story seems surprisingly apropos, when thinking about that plane load of survivors of the Khmer Rouge, and of the primitive "mountain people" wearing their shorts and carrying their bamboo.

It would be easy to laugh at them, and how they might have reacted to it all, but at the same time difficult to comprehend the culture shocks that awaited them, that they had to be experiencing every moment of the journey. In many respects, it is hard to see what kept them from being psychologically overwhelmed, unable to cope with it all.

None of that seemed to be an issue with Albert. He had spent enough time in Phnom Penh to be familiar with modern society and its gadgetry. The language barrier would pose problems for some time, but he managed to cope quite well with being suddenly transported out of the jungles of Cambodia and Thailand to the jungles of metropolitan America.

"It was so hot in Bangkok, but when we walked off the airplane, I think in San Francisco, these people handed us jackets. We never saw jackets, before. 'What are we to do with these things?' We couldn't understand why they put these huge 'shirts' on top of us. After that, we walked out of the airport, and it was a shock. Oh my goodness! Just so cold! Now we know what that heavy shirt is for. Then they fed us these hot noodles. I don't know what it was, but that was the best thing I ever had.

"After we had been there a while, I don't know how long, they loaded us again on the huge bus to take us to the airport. They told us everything, but nobody understood what they said. We don't know where they are taking us." In due time, however, he found himself on yet another "huge Boeing," enroute on the final leg of his flight, to his new home in Houston, Texas.

As is true in most other aspects of Albert's life and story, the significance is in the experience and not in the details, for he remembers few of them. He was not certain, for example, that his flight to America landed in San Francisco. But he is certain he arrived in California, and it was quite chilly—so it was unlikely that he arrived in balmy Los Angeles. But again—the details are not the story. What seems more significant was what must have been going through his mind during the many hours on the "huge Boeing" on the flight from Bangkok to California.

Try to imagine reversing the situation. Imagine yourself on a flight from California to Bangkok, to take up residence in Cambodia, never to live again in your native land. Surely, your mind would be in turmoil. Albert's mind surely must have been tumbling, during the long flight from Bangkok to the US, the brief time in San Francisco, and finally the flight to what was to become his new home in Houston, Texas. But in fact, Albert had few such thoughts about his future.

"No, I was just numb," he said. "My mind was just in shock. Everything was still too scary, the frightening times were still too real, to even think."

That was quite understandable, given his experiences—but his sense of humor was not dead.

"The flight was so funny," he said, suddenly taking a lighter note. "It kept me laughing. Those mountain people, they didn't know the civilized world, at all. During the flight, every time the flight attendants passed by, they kept asking for the little bottles of wine. They didn't know they were supposed to pay. The flight people, they just kept bringing it. The mountain people, they just about drank themselves half to death. But the airline people, they knew they were refugees, and they didn't say anything. They just let them have it. That was very nice, I think.

"Now, here is where it got embarrassing. While we were flying, they all lined up for the restrooms. Every time the airplane, what do you call it? Turbulence? Every time there was turbulence, they all grabbed hold of the seats, wrapped their legs around, holding on for dear life. They never felt anything like that. Then, when they go to the restroom, they don't know about how you flush. Oh my goodness. And they don't know how to sit on the toilet seat. They face the other way. But they don't know. They never saw anything like any of that, before. It was so embarrassing. But it was so funny."

It is quite possible that Albert's experiences on the plane, watching the mountain people trying to cope with modern life, may have been the first time he had laughed in six years of what he called his "darkness." Perhaps the experience was part of his healing, helping him rediscover some of the normal emotions of being human.

At long last, an airplane landed at Houston International Airport and a group of people, probably looking perplexed and apprehensive, walked down the jet-way and out of the terminal into a new life. It would be quite easy to imagine them standing on the curb, awaiting a ride that would take them they knew not where, looking uncertainly at the dizzying turmoil of a modern airport covered with indecipherable words, and wondering what, for sure, they had gotten into.

America is a land of immigrants. People like that have arrived on our shores from the time a group got out of a longboat on the shores of what would eventually become Virginia, and looked just as uncertainly at what was to become their new home. The settlers at Jamestown established a tradition honored for four hundred years. We welcome them home. And so it was for Albert Cheng. The USCC group had all arrangements prepared for him and the others.

"They had this apartment for the refugees," Albert said. "That was where I lived, at first. But I didn't know anyone, didn't speak the language. There was nothing much I could do. But there was a place called the YMCA. They had the classes for teaching you the language, learn the A,B,C,D. There were buses that came by, buses just keep coming up and down the street, all the time.

"But I wouldn't ride the bus, because I didn't know where they would be taking me," he recalled, laughing heartily at himself. "When it rains, walk in the rain. When it is cold, walk in the cold. I couldn't read the signs. I was afraid I would get lost, and never get back. So I always walked."

Given the unwillingness of so many who come to America to adapt to their new home and learn English, it is truly impressive that one of the first things Albert did on arrival here was to begin attending classes to learn the language. And how was that done? Did the YMCA have translators at those classes?

"No, they used pictures, they point, and say the word. Hair, nose, chair, airplane. They just keep showing us the pictures, making us say the word. After a while, we learned the words. The thing about me is, I repeat the word so I learn it better. And I am never afraid to ask 'What does this mean?' if I don't understand."

Of course, Albert had learned in French while in school in Cambodia and that background helped him as he had already been exposed to a second language structure.

"Yes," he agreed. "The French helped. For example, you have the same word, table, for where you eat. The French pronounce it a different way, but it is the same word.

"Another thing, at the United Nations camp, they taught English. I learned a lot of words, and I thought I would be okay. But oh my goodness, when I came to Texas and the Texas people began to speak, I didn't know a thing," he exclaimed, laughing with—or perhaps at—us Texans, with our funny words, like "fixin'" and "y'all."

"The first time I heard the word 'Dude,' like 'What's up, Dude?' I went to the dictionary to try to find the word 'dude.' Later on I learned there is such a thing as slang, and idioms. I thought, 'Oh my goodness! How will I ever learn English?'"

On the surface, it appeared that Albert was adapting pretty well to his new life in America. But as is sometimes said, looks can be deceiving. It was understandable. Albert had undergone nearly four years of brutal treatment and suffering, then two more years of uncertainty in the UN camps. He had no idea what had become of any of his family, or if any of them were alive. He had been transplanted to a country he had scarcely known existed, and was now trying to function day by day in a city as foreign to him as if he were living on Mars.

"Yes, I was getting along," he finally responded, "but I was very lonely, and homesick. I missed my family so much. I didn't even know if they were alive, or dead. And always, I cried for God. I had always thought Buddha was God, but in my heart I was always seeking God."

That God that Albert longed for, and was constantly seeking, had big things in store for His lost sheep, but the time had not yet come, and a move to Dallas would be required. Life took another big turn for Albert one day, when he received an unexpected phone call.

"Oh, yes, my friend called me," Albert said. "He was a Buddhist monk I met when we were at the United Nations camp, and we got acquainted. They asked us where we wanted to go when we left the camp. We don't have a clue. We know there is this place called 'Texas.' We saw in the movies about the cowboys. But we don't have a clue what Texas is. We don't even know how big the United States is. We just decided we would go to this place called Texas.

"When he called, I didn't know where he was. But somehow he got a phone number for me, and one day he called me. He said he called so many times, he didn't know how many times he called. But about the phone calls, I was so scared to pick up the phone because if somebody spoke the English, I didn't understand it. But of course, he spoke Khmer, so we could talk. I couldn't believe it when he called me.

"He said, 'Why don't you come to Dallas, and live here? We will come get you.' I think, *Okay. I'll move to Dallas.* The whole car load, they just loaded up in the car and came and got me. It was so funny. If you tell them turn on this street, and this and that, they can never get the name of the street. If you say the name of a street, they don't know where they are. But if you say, 'There is a big tree on the corner, there is a big building,' they get it. I just stayed with the phone, and said, 'Keep on coming, keep on coming...there is a tall building...look at the numbers.' It took us <u>all</u> day to run into each other, but somehow they found me. Then, wow, we are standing there face to face, and we recognize each other. It was the first time for a long time that I could speak my language again...and smell the rice again. I couldn't eat the hamburger, then. Oh my goodness....

"Somehow, he got a job for me in The Episcopal Church of the Good Shepherd, in Dallas. I packed my stuff, and they brought me to Dallas. And that is how I began working in the church. I have to say, it was God who put me there, because my heart fits so well with kind people, gentle people," he said.

So Albert rejoiced with his friends. One can only imagine the pace of the conversation as the car sped them northward. He was probably happier than he had been in the previous six years. Lurking below the surface of all those emotions, though, constantly tormenting him, were the nightmares, the indelible memories of horrors that couldn't be erased. He would continue to seek peace, turning again to the Buddha he had always known as God—even though Buddha said he was not God—turning to his meditations, always seeking, always asking, "Where is God? Is there a God?"

That seeking, those questions, were going to be answered for Albert in ways he could not have imagined. But the answers were not to be found where he expected them. For those answers, he was led to a Presbyterian church in Richardson, Texas.

Chapter 8

Amazing Grace

For the Son of man came to seek out and to save the lost.
Luke 19:10

And so, it might have appeared, the saga of Cheng Sopanarith was coming to a close. He had survived the atrocities of the Khmer Rouge, escaped, had come to America and had become Albert Cheng. He had been found by friends, was now joining them, and was ready to start a new life of peacefulness. His life could then have gone for him in a similar fashion as it often does for combat veterans who return home at the conclusion of a war.

All too often, veterans survive the horrors of war and come back home, ready to get back to normal and start their lives over again. On the surface, all might appear to be going well for them. But within many are dark, disturbing memories that cause many of those "peaceful" lives to be Thoreau's "...lives of quiet desperation." They struggle with nightmares, with flashbacks of experiences that won't leave them in peace. But they keep it all bottled inside, never letting the demons out. And many suffer the consequences.

And so it was with Albert. He was eager to put his painful past in the trash bin of history, forget it, leave it all behind in far-away

Cambodia. Life was peaceful in America, and peace was what he had been seeking all his life. He would get a job, learn the language, become a citizen. Life would be good. Albert Cheng made a valiant effort to lead such a life of peace. But the demons within him were not ready to give up the battle.

That battle for his mind, heart and soul would rage for years within him, largely unseen by those around him, and was not to be won until he was led down a path that he could never have imagined. The journey down that path, a journey to a rendezvous with the cross, the "wood" that he had seen in the movie at the refugee camp but did not understand, started with the trip from Houston, up I-45 to Dallas.

After a day-long exercise in playing "Marco, Polo" over the telephone, Albert's heart had leapt with joy as he saw the car driven by his Cambodian friend come to a stop in front of his apartment. After many hugs and tears—and a meal at the closest spot serving rice—they were loaded in the car, driving northbound through the urban sprawl that is Houston, Texas. Albert was headed for yet another chapter in his new life in America, in Dallas, Texas. A sponsor with The Episcopal Church of the Good Shepherd in Dallas had arranged a place for Albert to live, and had lined up a job as custodian at the church for him.

"God seemed to always put me in a Christian church," Albert commented as he remembered those early days. He later took a similar job at The Episcopal Church of the Epiphany, in Richardson, Texas, a nearby suburb of Dallas.

Albert continued to adapt to his new life, his new country and its stupefying, complex language full of all those strange words, like "Dude." Days of routine turned into months, and months into years. All in all, it appeared on the surface that the horrors of his previous life were fading. But there were still many twists and turns to come in the plot of Albert's life.

The friend who had rescued him from Houston, the Buddhist monk he had met so many years ago, had more in store for Albert and introduced him to his wife's cousin, Sineth. In due time, she and Albert were married. His list of "firsts" continued to grow, as he added first-time home owner to being a newly-wed husband. In 1987, "first-time father" was added to his list, when their daughter, Connie, was born. As though all those new experiences were not enough, Albert wanted to become an official citizen of the new country that had adopted him; citizenship became his goal.

On April 12, 1989, Albert raised his right hand, repeated the oaths read to him, and became an American citizen. Somehow, it would have been even more meaningful if the ceremony could have been five days later, as April 17 was the anniversary of the fall of Phnom Penh, the event that resulted in Albert becoming an American citizen. Whatever the date, becoming an American citizen was a joyous affair for Albert and his friends, and appeared to close the book on his life as a Cambodian. Two years later, Connie got a little brother, Johnny.

It appeared—and was generally assumed by those around him—that Albert had finally put the past and its nightmares behind him. Indeed, very few knew any of what the quiet, private Cambodian had been through. Time heals all wounds, we often say. But some wounds take longer to heal than others, and we are more than what people see on the surface. All was not well in Albert's life. The memories had not faded, the nightmares were not over. Albert had yet to find the God that would give him the peace he constantly sought.

"One night, years ago, I was driving through Richardson," he remembered, "and it flashed through my mind, it all came back. I didn't have control. I think I was just too deeply wounded—the frightening times, the deep, deep scary moments, the hurt. I thought, *Oh no, it's happening all over again, the past.* I had no control. I began to just weep, and weep, I couldn't think, I just kept driving. Red lights? I didn't even see them. I just drove, weeping, tears streaming down. I couldn't stop.

"Then two Richardson police stopped me. Oh, they were so angry. So angry. I had no control, I couldn't stop weeping. They made me get in the back of their car. They couldn't understand it. I just couldn't stop the tears. Of course, they couldn't understand me. I was talking in Khmer. And I was too upset to understand them."

What the two policemen, who were simply trying to do their job, could not have known, could not have comprehended, was what was behind the inconsolable crying of their "perp," babbling in the back seat in an incomprehensible language. In their world, crying was probably for babies and sissies. For Albert, at that moment, it was an incredible release, a catharsis.

"It was the only opportunity I had since I was captured to cry," Albert confessed. "I like to cry. I feel good when I cry. It's a release. And the Communists? No way. Tears were a sign to them that you were unhappy with your life in Communism, and that meant you were the enemy. You cry, and you get killed, maybe, or tortured. When a pistol, an AK-47 points at you, there's just no way. I had to stuff the tears back in, all those years."

The facade that was Albert's smiling mask was beginning to crack, as his new life was anything but peaceful. His mind and soul were full of turmoil that he could no longer "stuff back," as he had done with his tears for so many years.

"With freedom, a wife and family, I thought everything was okay," he related. "But there was a darkness in me. I kept asking, 'Where is God? What is God? Is Buddha God?'"

The need for inner peace, for his soul to be in harmony with the God that he could neither identify nor find, a search that began in the jungle as a child with his Uncle Hank, had never been satisfied, his thirst never slaked. And another problem was brewing. Without being fully aware of it, he had lost all his anchors in life.

First, his home and family in Cambodia had been the anchor of his youth. He was by nature a peaceful, trusting person. He was oriented toward the spiritual, and found meditation easy and fulfilling. His life as a Buddhist was accepted, and held in high regard. He had great respect for the Buddha, the monks and temples. There was no basis in his life for doubting, or questioning.

Then came the Khmer Rouge, and he lost it all. He had no knowledge of his family, if they had even survived. His faith in his fellow man, his spiritual beliefs, were shaken to their foundations.

"When I see something that I was used to for so long, and have such great respect for, when I see the Communists, the Khmer Rouge, come right into the temple and execute the monks, right in front of the Golden Buddha in the temple, to see things that we hold in such great respect, and is so good, yet turn out to be the most horrible, horrible thing, how the Communists execute even the monks who we respect most high…when I see all of that, I was just completely…lost.

"I realized the Golden Buddha had no power, no power whatsoever. That is why I was just completely lost. Yet, I saw miracles along through the jungle. One of the things we still believe in is the ancestor. We think our ancestors are still with us. During my escape, running through the mines and bullets, I see in my mind the dream. I see the people dressed in the white cloth. I remember, I think, *Oh, that must be my great-great-grandmother. She is leading me through all the minefields.* That was the old thinking, the old culture. That was the thinking I was taught.

"It is amazing, now that I have come to read the Bible, it was the same form and shape as the angels. Now that I have come to know the Word, reading the Bible, I have no doubt in my mind. It was an angel who was leading me, walked with me, went with me, all along. At that point, the picture of the Buddha was gone. After the Khmer executed the monks, all the blood in the temple, in my mind the picture of the Buddha was gone. But then, I didn't know, I didn't have the Word. But I think that was when I began to feel the spiritual aspect of things.

"I was so fed up with people, with the man systems. All those things were still inside of me. I was losing the trust. I didn't trust people anymore. People (Khmer Rouge 'meeting leaders') would tell me the phrase to say, and all those things, but I didn't sense the sincerity of people anymore. I didn't sense the truth in people anymore. After seeing all that, it kept reminding me that no matter what, people are cruel to each other. And that's when I began my spiritual journey, the spiritual aspects."

But where do we turn when we've lost our way, when we have been cast adrift with no shore in sight, just vast expanses of nothingness? Many of us turn to drink, to drugs, trying to lose ourselves because we are lost. But Albert could not give up on his spiritual quest. He had to find that true source of strength and faith in his life. He had no where else to turn, so he turned again to his roots. He returned to the Buddhism of his youth.

"One Friday night after work I went to the Khmer temple, the Cambodian temple in Dallas, and I start the old thing again—fast and pray, fast and pray. I felt deeply wounded, and traumatized, inside. It felt like there is nothing in the world but to suffer. And I didn't know anything about my family, Mother and Father, my brothers and sisters. So I spent most of my time meditating. Night and day, longing and seeking."

It wasn't working. As Albert put it, "I was seeking God with a capital G and no matter where I turned, I felt just as lost." The more he attempted to return to his Buddhist faith the more desperate he became—and the more lost he felt. There seemed to be no where to look, no one to turn to. Habit, or perhaps desperation, kept returning him to his Buddhist roots but finally, even that began to ring hollow.

"This was an eye opener for me. One night I went to the Buddhist temple, and asked to go inside the temple so I can sit there and meditate. The Buddhist Satva there told me, 'You can go ahead, but I am not going to go in the temple, at night.' I asked him, 'Why not?' He said, 'There is a ghost in there at night.'

"I think, oh sheesh," Albert said, having to stop and laugh at the memory. "I think, I am longing for God and I come to the place where there is supposed to be God, and instead of God in the temple, there is the ghost. I am so confused and I am so seeking for the truth, and at the same time I am so sick of this farce, this untruth. I go where there is supposed to be the big G and the big G turns out to be ghost instead of god. I just felt lost, again. Then I said, 'Okay, I am going in the temple, anyway. And I go in, and there are four old ladies in the temple, and they are sleeping head to head. They are scared of the ghost. So I meditate all night, all night. But I didn't get into a spiritual sense. There was just confusion, confusion. All these things that were inside of me, I couldn't deal with it."

But what Albert could not know was that the "God with a capital G" that he was seeking was also seeking him. Angels began to be placed in Albert's life. The first angel was in the form of a good-hearted, impulsive woman named Marna Brown. At that time, in early 1992, Marna was Director of the Discovery School operated by Canyon Creek Presbyterian Church in Richardson, Texas.

The church was in need of a new custodian. Hiring and firing of church staff was not part of her job description, but impulsive Marna took it on herself to begin calling other churches in the area. Her very first call was to a member of the nearby Episcopal Church of the Epiphany.

'Oh, we made such a big mistake,' Marna remembers the member lamenting during that call. 'We decided for financial reasons to let our custodian go and begin using a commercial service. He was a Cambodian, and was so friendly. His name was Albert Cheng.'

Marna quickly got his phone number and called Albert, interviewed him, and got the church officials to hire him.

"It worked out well," Marna recalled. "Albert had always assumed most of the responsibilities for their two small children, and would often bring them to work with him. Of course, they fit right into our day care facilities."

And Albert fit right in with the children of the church school. He loved playing with them, and they loved him. He took every opportunity to play on the playground with them, to climb on the church roof or scamper up the playground equipment to amuse them. They flocked around him like goslings around Mother Goose. But sometimes his enthusiasm and eagerness to entertain the children went a bit too far.

"Someone would come to me saying that Albert was squirting the children in the hallway with a water pistol, or was up on the church roof pretending to be a monkey," Marna recalled. "I would have to call him in and tell him, 'Albert, you just can't do things like that. The kids want to do it too, and we can't let them.' Of course, the children loved it, and loved Albert for doing it."

The innocence and loving nature of the children were therapeutic for Albert, but even that was not sufficient to heal his inner wounds or cleanse his mind and soul of the anguish he felt. He was still a troubled man.

"He came to us knowing almost no English," recalls the minister of the church at that time, the Reverend Jack Noble. "My primary recollection of Albert at the time was of a terribly 'beaten' person, who very quietly and singularly went about his work with great dignity. He would on occasion bring his dear little daughter, and at times his wife would come to help. Whenever she came, their little boy would come as well. But for the most part Albert would be there alone working very diligently. Because of his lack of English, and my non-existent Cambodian, we would not talk at any great length, until after he had been with us for two or three years. And then I remember him as being very curious about us Christians. At times, I would come by late in the evening and he would sometimes be there in the quiet, in prayer or meditation."

Marna was his compass, his rock, during these increasingly troubled times, for Albert. He often turned to her for guidance and support.

"We had a good relationship," Marna said. "We became friends, and I cared about him a lot. But as time passed, Albert began to have problems, especially in his marriage to Sineth. At first, I had no idea of all that he had experienced, or what he was going through. But later on, I began to be aware that he was a deeply troubled man. He literally had demons fighting inside of him."

Age and cultural differences, as well as personality differences, between Albert and Sineth all were taking their toll.

Ultimately the marriage failed. A time came when Albert moved out of the house he had purchased when they got married. Marna and her husband, John, were aware that all was not well with their new friend.

"One night we were driving home," Marna related. "It was a dank, cold, rainy night. I said, 'John, I'm concerned about Albert. I feel we should go check on him.' So we went by the church. We found him there, hauling in one of the big garbage containers. I asked him, 'Albert, where are you staying tonight?' He was sort of vague."

Albert insisted that all was fine with him, that he was coping. But Marna wasn't persuaded, and pressed him for more details.

"I found out that he had been stringing a hammock up in the trees at the church, and sleeping there. Or sometimes, he would sleep on some of the couches."

That was too much for Albert's angel of mercy, and at the insistence of John and Marna he moved into their guest bedroom. It was at the Browns' each morning that Albert began to be exposed to the meaning of Christianity, and the tug-of-war with his lifelong, cultural belief in Buddhism began.

"John and I had a ritual of reading some scripture after breakfast, and then talking about it. Albert began to join in, and would sometimes ask questions," Marna said. "We didn't know it, but he would go back into his bedroom afterward and do his meditation and worship of Buddha."

"I am amazed that God let me 'shop around' for so long," Albert commented about the experiences, many years later. In spite of having worked in Christian churches since he arrived in Richardson, the lifelong cultural grip of Buddhism wouldn't release him.

Nevertheless, the influence of living with the Browns, and his daily exposure to Christianity where he worked, all continued to plant seeds. Those seeds were taking root, but grew slowly.

The fertile soil that first let those seeds begin to grow, that let the healing begin, was the mentoring influence and friendship that quickly developed with John and Marna. For the first time, Albert began to be able to open up about what he had suffered.

"At first, I didn't know about any of what had happened to him," Marna said. "None of us did. But day by day, Albert would come to me for help with the many problems of dealing with modern society, with the banks, the credit card companies, all those mysterious letters that would appear in his mailbox. In fact, he began to refer to me as his mother. Eventually, Albert began to share with me some of his years of captivity."

An event that occurred in 1996 was pivotal for Albert, in many ways. For all the years since he had escaped and come to America, Albert knew essentially nothing about the fate of his family. He became more and more desperate to finally get to return and learn what he could, and get to see whatever members of his family he could find. Again, the Browns stepped in to help.

"Albert wanted to go back to Cambodia," Marna recalled. "So I appealed to the congregation, and everybody donated to help him pay for a ticket. Finally, the sanctuary was packed, and I told everybody that Albert was finally going to be able to return to Cambodia and see his "jungle brother." Of course, everybody was so happy for him. Later on, I thought, *He isn't going to be able to see his jungle brother.* He wouldn't even be able to know where he lived. So John asked him, 'Albert, how are you going to be able to find your jungle brother?' Albert laughed at him and said, 'Not jungle brother—younger brother.' I'll bet that whole congregation went home wondering how on earth he was going to find a brother in the jungle."

The trip was excruciatingly painful at times and overwhelmingly joyful at others. but served as an essential step toward healing for Albert.

"As the airplane was coming into the Phnom Penh airport, and I looked down on that city where I had suffered so much pain, seen so much that I wanted to forget, all the old feelings, the fear, just came flooding back," Albert recalled. "I just about couldn't face it, at first. As we were driving along one road, there was this sudden flash of memory. I thought, *This is where I ran across, when I was trying to escape*. All those memories…it was very hard, for me."

The trip was not all painful, though. Call it fate, if you will, or God's grace, but Albert found his "jungle brother."

"I was walking along this path, out in the countryside, among the rice fields," Albert related the story. "Down the path, I saw a man walking toward me, wearing the Cambodian hat. As he got closer, he stopped, and we just stood and looked at each other. Then I said, 'Bong?'—that is the term we use to greet each other, that means like being a brother—'Bong, is that you?' I could not believe my eyes. This man was my little brother. He was just a boy, when I last saw him. It was such a joyful time, for us."

That joy, though heartfelt, was tempered by the fact that Albert learned of the fate of his parents, and the other family members who had been executed. It was also on this trip when Albert began to learn more of the extent of the atrocities that had flooded over his country. By that time, some of the Khmer Rouge prisons had been turned into museums, and far more had been learned of the mass executions and burials of the Killing Fields.

"When Albert returned from Cambodia, we invited him and his family to go with us to Minnesota for our annual vacation at our lake cabin up there," Marna remembered. "He had with him this photo album of just the darkest, most gruesome pictures from over there. Pictures of piles of bones from the Killing Fields, of prisons where people were tortured. I think maybe that was a cleansing for him. But I thought, *Albert, you don't need to dwell on this stuff.* He wanted to show it to my whole family, over and over and over again."

Whatever effect his trip, and the exposure to the gruesome stories and pictures, may have had on Albert one thing was certain. The influence of working with people like Marna and John, and the staff and members of Canyon Creek Presbyterian Church, was steadily opening him to healing.

"When I began to work at Canyon Creek," he said, "I saw people that were more sincere, and I would think, *These people smile all the time. Why do the Christians smile so much?* I began to see the things I knew in the past. I saw the gentleness, the sweetness of the people. I somehow began to learn how to trust again, because people seemed to be more sincere. It began to slightly move me into the process of healing."

That process of healing was further aided by Marna helping Albert face his painful past, and learn to better deal with it. Part of that healing came from gaining the strength to begin to share his experiences with the public.

"At one point," Marna continued, "I helped him write up a short testimonial of his experiences, that he later shared with the church. Later on, he was interviewed on a local radio station and by the newspaper. But that was mostly after his conversion, and he was far better able to deal with it all."

It was about this same time that God put another angel in Albert's life, in the person of Mary Hodge, then Director of Children's Ministries at Canyon Creek Presbyterian Church.

"God put another angel in my life, and that angel's name was Mary," Albert insisted, smiling at the memory of it. "She began to share the scriptures with me, and I shared the Sanskrit (the centuries-old language of Buddhism) with her. I tried to see, tried to balance these new scriptures with the Sanskrit. It was the first time in my life that I began to have the Word of God right in front of my face. It was what I had longed for, had been seeking. And she began to share with me. The one thing I can say about Mary is that I can say anything, can ask anything, and she just sits there and listens," he laughed. "She was just so open. She helped me begin to trust people, a bit at a time."

"I joined the Canyon Creek Presbyterian Church staff in 1993, as Director of Children's Ministries," Mary elaborated. "Albert had been on staff since March 1, 1992, as custodian. I thought Albert was a Christian because he was always so nice, polite, kind, and helpful. One day—maybe in 1997—it occurred to me that he might like help reading the Bible since his English was limited. I offered to read the Bible with him. He agreed and we began to meet during our lunch break. We would find an empty classroom and read for about an hour one to three times a week.

"I chose to begin with the Gospel of John since that's the portion of scripture that Billy Graham gave to new converts during his evangelistic crusades. During our conversations, Albert mentioned that he still had some Buddhist ways and beliefs. I said, 'That's OK.' I surmised that transitioning from Buddhism to Christianity would take time. I believe this is why Albert says I was patient with him. He refers to me as an angel, and I do believe that God sent me as His messenger—which is what an angel is. It was totally God's doing."

It is Albert's belief that sharing the scriptures with the Browns and with Mary Hodge, seeing the open friendliness and trusting nature of the people at the churches, were preparing him, beginning to open his heart and mind, getting him ready for the "Big Event." In spite of all that, however, Albert was not yet ready to yield, to give up on his former faith.

"Even though I may express myself in a Christian way, in my heart I was not. I kept wearing my mask, pretending like I am one of the Christians, too. But I don't even have a clue. People would ask me, 'How are you?' and I say 'Just fine, I'm doing just fine.' But inside? No way."

That was all about to change.

"One night at John and Marna Brown's house, where I was staying, the history of the new life began. I bowed down and worshipped the Buddha, as usual, doing the chanting, the thousand years of the language, the Sanskrit of the chant. After that I lay down to go to sleep, and then I see the cross. It still doesn't mean anything to me. Does it have a meaning? Nothing. It has no meaning to me whatsoever. But I see this huge cross, floating in the sky. I look at the cross. It still has no meaning. I laugh at it. Right after I worship the Buddha, the cross shows up. Then this incredible sheet of light, the kind of light I experienced one time when lightning hit the transformer by the church and this ball of fire—Boooosh!—just blinded my eyes for several seconds. This kind of light blaze, incredible. I smash my head, and I pass out. Then this blaze of light, incredible light, beautiful light, rises up beside me in the form of a human. But I still don't know the meaning. It is too much for me to handle, all of this. I can't look at the light with the naked eye, it is too much.

"Then the song began. This beautiful song began. It is not an earthly voice, it is the voice of the angels, singing inside of me, from inside my heart. Then the most incredible moment of my life, that I never ever experienced, this incredible peace. After that I got the Webster Dictionary and tried to look up the word "peace," to find the whole meaning of it. It comes down to this: I can ask the meaning of the word in English, and I can ask the meaning in Cambodian. The best thing I can say is this: it is indescribable.

"When you are encountering this peace it is not just the meaning of the word, the vital part is that it is this life of peace, the life of Jesus. Peace is not just a word, it is the life of Jesus inside of me. This is the nature of God. That is the kind of peace I was looking for when I was at the temple. In Buddhism, I tried to earn that. It turned out to be a gift, a gift from God.

"I had been wearing the mask of anger, the mask of revenge, the mask of the wounded, all these masks. At the moment of God's presence...gone! All these masks, just gone. Then it seemed like I was floating in space. I drew a picture of what I had seen, to help share it. At that moment, I felt my body was floating in space. And the restoring, the healing, began. I remember when I went to see a psychiatrist, he gave me this long list to check, check, check. He gave me the bottles of pills. But all the terrible moments of the past happened all over again. Not even the power of the medicine could keep it away. But then I came to understand that healing is all in the power of God.

"This is so funny. I had worked all day, my body was exhausted. After all those incredible things going on, the body tried to fight back. I looked at the clock. One o'clock. I go back to sleep again. But it was like in the movie. Here comes Part II. That incredible moment came back. I don't want to let go, just be in it. I could care less about anything else, at that moment, it meant so much to me. My heart, at that point...I'm in a different place.

"Anyway, at dawn, I tried to look back in my spirit, I am overjoyed, overwhelmed, it was just flooding all over. It's amazing. I can't describe it. When I got to work that morning I ran to Pam Miller (Music Director, at the time, for the Discovery School of Canyon Creek Presbyterian Church). I asked her about the song, the music I heard. She said, 'Why don't you sing it?' Oh my, icy moment. As a Buddhist, I can chant the Sanskrit. But I don't sing. I do not sing. Then all of a sudden, the Holy Spirit got a hold of me, I just sang it out. I think, *How did that happen? That was not me.*

"Then she turned to me, and she said, 'Albert. That's "Amazing Grace." Don't you know it?' I said, 'No, I don't.' She told me, 'It's Hymn 280 in our hymnal.' I ran into the sanctuary, grabbed a hymnal and looked it up. I read every word, and they jumped into my heart. And I was just weeping, weeping. It was the first time (since the Richardson Police episode) that I enjoyed crying. Later on, I walked to the office of Dr. Lewis (Donald Gordon Lewis, Jr., pastor of the church). I told him, 'I want to get baptized.' I don't even know what baptism is. Whatever happened to me that night, I know that Person walked with me all along. It was Him."

"I was aware, when I came to Canyon Creek, of Albert's circumstance," Dr. Lewis said of the time, "but I had few details. I knew Mary (Hodge) was working with him, teaching him the scriptures and the story of salvation. At one point, Albert came to me, and asked to be baptized. I talked with him, and with Mary. We filled out a Baptism form to present to the Session. I remember kneeling on the floor of my office with him, and thanking God for being at work in Albert's life, and for this moment of conversion.

"Over the years, Albert had become a beloved member of the staff, and was loved by the congregation. There was some awareness at the time of the effect of that conversion on his home life, and on his wife and her family, and the cost of that. Our church had a series of Stewardship meetings at about that time, and

Albert stood and gave his first testimony. Because of his experiences and the dramatic nature of his conversion, and his halting use of English, the congregation paid rapt attention. He had learned to play the guitar, and sang "Amazing Grace." It was an especially moving time for our church."

On February 22, 1998—some twenty years after his escape from the Khmer Rouge—Albert Cheng stood at the Baptismal Font at the front of the sanctuary of Canyon Creek Presbyterian Church and was baptized into his new faith.

"At first, I was very suspect of Albert's conversion," Marna Brown said of that time. "Albert was so eager to please us. There was an element to him of 'I'll do anything to please you,' at that time. In a sense, he was so eager to please that he was, at times, sort of a yes-man. I was concerned that he was doing this just so he could seem to be one of us, now. He was smiling a lot. I thought, 'That could be real, but it might not.' I was very skeptical, at first. But it didn't take long before I knew it was real. You'd find him in the sanctuary, praying. He was always wanting to meet Mary, to learn more about the scriptures. He would come over here and talk with John. But I think, had it not been for being able to talk to Mary, and get so well grounded so quickly, like that…well, who knows. For someone in her position, to take the time to talk like that with a custodian of the church? That says a lot—about the church, and about who Mary is."

So, the seeker had been sought, and found. The barefoot boy who had climbed the tallest trees on the highest hills in the jungle to get to be closer to whatever spirit resided out there, up there, the survivor who had carried his demons with him from the Killing Fields to the Land of the Free, had finally found peace. He had won his battle. Or so it seemed, after his joyous conversion experience and baptism.

Demons are worthy foes, however, and don't give up on us easily. Although Albert had found, or been found by, his Lord and Savior there were still battles to be fought. It was during those battles with his inner demons, battles that occurred on several different occasions in his bedroom, in a serene state park, at the church, that Albert felt he had in fact finally lost the battle, had finally been conquered by all the evil in his life. The demons were literally killing him. But he now had a new protector. His "God with a capital G" was with him, as He had been through all that had gone before—but Albert had not known, then, of his benefactor.

Sketch by Albert depicting his amazing conversion experience, and first hearing the hymn *Amazing Grace*. The verse from Galatians 2:20 reads, in part, "...it is no longer I who live, but Christ who lives in me."

Albert's illustration of how he was constantly haunted by nightmares of his persecution, and how he had to keep his eye on the cross. In Luke 9:62, Jesus states that "No one who puts his hand to the plow and looks back is fit for the kingdom of God."

Chapter 9

The Final Battle

Now, the word of the Lord came to Jonah...saying, "Arise, go to Nineveh, that great city, and cry against it; for their wickedness has come up before me."

Jonah 1:1-2

And he healed many who were sick with various diseases, and cast out many demons; and he would not permit the demons to speak, because they knew him.

Mark 1:34

The Book of Jonah in the Old Testament of the Bible presents a rather thought-provoking story, the oft-told tale of Jonah and the whale. The book is quite short—containing just four chapters on two pages. But in those four chapters, and the story of Jonah, many of the aspects—both good and bad—of Man's relationship with God are revealed.

In brief, in the story God has grown most displeased with the people of the great city of Nineveh, for they have become quite wicked in their ways. God speaks to Jonah, directing him to go to Nineveh and "cry against it," calling on the people of the city to repent. Otherwise, God is going to destroy them and their city.

But Jonah is offended by their wicked ways and has no sympathy for them. Frankly, he would prefer to see them destroyed. Simply stated, Jonah was unwilling to perform the mission God had for him and put up a considerable struggle against it. He did what most of us do in such a situation—he ran the other way. Of course, he suffered some unpleasant consequences as a result—you may have heard the story of him being swallowed by the whale. Of course, God ultimately prevailed. Jonah was delivered to Nineveh, the people listened and repented, and Nineveh was saved.

Perhaps it's a stretch, but in a sense that story seems applicable to Albert following his conversion experience. Jonah was a good man, chosen by God for a mission. Albert was a good man, and as it turned out was also chosen by God for a mission. Albert would not become aware of that mission for several years, but his "Nineveh" was to be his own home country of Cambodia, a country where wickedness had been elevated to an art form and in dire need of a message of salvation.

Like Jonah, Albert was not yet ready for such a mission. Certainly, he was not ready to offer a message of salvation to the demonic forces of the Khmer Rouge. His inner desire was to return someday armed not with a message of salvation, but with an AK-47 to kill as many of them as possible. He had his own demons to contend with, and in his own way struggled as Jonah did. But his struggle was to finally be released from the forces of darkness and evil that seemed to possess him.

With our penchant for rationality and disdain for anything that hints at the occult, Albert's struggle took on manifestations that are difficult for many of us from Western cultures to comprehend. We read of Jesus casting out demons, but somehow want to believe that what He really did was to cure a rather severe case of epilepsy, or perhaps seizures—or something. Satan, casting out demons, all that stuff couldn't possibly be real—could it? The Western world is inclined to assign belief in such things as being possessed by demons to the occult, or perhaps to "radical religionists."

For Albert, though, his coming battles were with demons that were as real to him as the Khmer Rouge had been. Those ghastly presences were not the product of an overactive imagination born of a culture of spirit worship. Once he had accepted Christ as his new savior, the battle was on. But he had been made partner with a powerful new Advocate, the Triune God: the Father, His Son, Jesus Christ, and the Holy Spirit.

"Okay, now that I received all of that," he said of the experiences, "it doesn't mean I am all perfectly healed, because we are still dealing with an imperfect world, right? The other side of it is the darkness. This is something I don't expect everyone to understand. It is just me. Because during the war, my body was controlled by all kinds of these other masters, either monks who deal with rituals, or the Khmer Rouge who are dealing with slashing the back, who did all kinds of stuff to me. I didn't realize, in my mind I still belonged to the old master because he got me from the first. And now, the battle began."

God knew that Albert would need all the help he could get, and put yet another angel in his path. This time, the angel was another Cambodian transplant to America. Although Albert loved his new Christian friends, and was joyful over his new-found faith, he still felt alone and missed his own culture, missed being able to hear and speak his own language.

"Things began to fall into place," Albert recalled, "and that is how I met Chheng Nuon. This is another example of God's hand. When I became a Christian, I could hardly believe that I had become a Christian. I sure couldn't believe there could be such a thing as another Cambodian Christian in Dallas. Then one night I was out driving, and it was raining. I saw this little sign in a shopping center, that said something about Cambodian Christian. I stopped, and wrote down the phone number.

"I called the number, and it turned out to be Chheng Nuon. He picked up the phone, and I said 'I see the sign Cambodian Christian. Does that have anything to do with you?' He said, 'Yes. Why don't you come on over?' So I drove to his house and went in. They were sitting on the floor, in a circle. It was the first time I saw the Khmer Bible. And they sit there, and they sing the songs. I think, *Hmm. So they sing the Christian songs. How about that?*"

Chheng was living in Garland, another suburb of Dallas, where Albert was also living at the time. He was trying to start a church there, but his vision was to return to Cambodia and plant a church in his home country. Chheng began to disciple Albert in the Christian faith. Because he spoke Khmer, he was able to make more progress than using English. Chheng had the Khmer Bible and used a curriculum called Theological Education by Extension, which gave a systematic approach to theology. It is somewhat of a "fill-in-the-blank" form of study, with the "answers in the back," but was an excellent learning tool for Albert at that stage.

"Albert was like a starving man who had been given bread; a thirsty man who had found water. Indeed, he had found, or rather been found by, the Bread of Life and the Living Water, even Jesus Christ," Mary Hodge said of him.

"The Lord God, He led Chheng Nuon into my life," Albert said. "He just came along, and treated me with the Word. One day, as soon as he got to know me closer and closer, he came into my house. It still bothered him when he walked into my house that there is the whole altar full of my Golden Buddha, and all sorts of other stuff. It must have bothered him so much. He come in to share the Word, and there is all that Golden Buddha and stuff—

must have been a couple of thousand dollars of stuff. All this stuff that I worship night and day, night and day.

"See, I was still in the darkness spirit. When the darkness spirit grabs hold of you, you have no power whatsoever. One day, before he left, he said, 'Why don't you take all that stuff and burn 'em?' I think, *Whoa!* This stuff is like life and death, very special to Buddhism. It has very great respect.

"So he left, and I think, *Okay.* I grabbed the whole thing. I lived in Garland at that time, and they have those plastic containers you put trash in. I packed the whole thing inside the container, and took it outside in the backyard, and I light it. Then I walked back inside. In not long, my house was surrounded by fire trucks and an ambulance. A neighbor called, they think my house is on fire. The fireman looked over the fence and he said, 'You okay? Are you barbequing, or something?' I say, 'Yes, I just barbeque.' So they left. I think, *I just barbequed the Buddha.*"

That line may be good for a laugh, but was in fact deeply profound. Theravada Buddhism has reigned over every facet of Cambodian life for longer than Christianity has existed. It is difficult to find a parallel in American life. No one factor so dominates our society and culture—not religion, not patriotism, nor any other "-ism"—as Cambodian society reflects its Buddhist roots. For Albert to "barbeque the Buddha" has no equivalent in our Western culture—unless, perhaps, it would be giving up television, or cell phones. Cavalier as it perhaps sounds, Albert was turning his back on his roots, his ancestors, on core beliefs trained into him since birth. Still, the war was not yet won.

"That night, I went for a walk, and came back and sat on my couch," Albert continued. "It was summer time, and very hot, maybe a hundred degrees. But I remember, at that moment I was freezing cold. Suddenly, my whole body was tossed right off the couch. I could see myself, kneeling in front of where the altar had been. And the battle began. The darkness, the force…later on, I understand the word, 'Satan.' That is what it is. Later on, I learned that when you or I are facing a darkness, a force, we are powerless, have no power whatsoever.

"Then I heard myself saying, 'Even though I am kneeling, I no longer worship you. I worship the new God. His name is Jesus. I no longer worship you.' And then it seemed like the whole house was fighting, fighting, and I was so exhausted. I think, *I've got to work tomorrow.* And my conscious mind thinks, *What's going on? Why is all this happening?* I lay down on the couch again, and that is the first time I learn how to pray. I know it is not me, but the Lord who is in me. But at the same time, I say to myself, 'Oh Lord. God. I've got to work tomorrow. And I am too tired. Could you put me back to sleep? Too much for me to handle, all this stuff. I'm too tired.'

"I remember clearly, at that point, the name of Jesus came in my mind. And the whole thing was just…gone. Left me. Gone! And then I sleep like a baby. Wake up in the morning, go to work. The experience is this, the thing I want to share. I hope that you never experience such a thing. But when you encounter such a darkness, a force, the Lord of Hosts is always there, even at the point of death. When I was facing that, completely in the hand of the darkness, I couldn't think of anything. I could do nothing. I tried to remember scripture. Nothing. Zero. Because of the darkness. I learned that the One [Jesus] who is in you and me, He was the One who did the battle for me. It was Him! Some people think they do that on their own. They don't realize, inside is the Most Almighty One. That's what I learned from that.

"The point is, the Lord wants to teach me that I don't have to find my way, do this thing like Buddhism, anymore. And that's why I came out of it. I tried to cast out the demons, do all those things on my own strength. But, no, no, no. The Lord showed me clearly. He handles everything!"

It was Post Traumatic Stress Syndrome, causing him to hallucinate to rid his mind of all the evil he had experienced. It was his Animist background, a result of growing up in a society that still believes that rocks and trees have spirits. We from Western cultures have all sorts of explanations for such experiences, willing to believe anything but what Albert insists was happening: God and Satan were battling for his soul. Albert now knew that with such an all-powerful Advocate, not even Satan could prevail. But Satan is a powerful force, not disposed to easily giving up the fight. There was more to come.

"I remember," Marna Brown said of Albert's battles with his internal demons, "one night my son got a call from the church (Canyon Creek Presbyterian). The school nurse was there. Albert was in really bad straits. My son, and John, went to the church. They literally had to hold Albert down while they prayed over him, praying for him to be delivered from the battles going on inside of him."

"Not just one time, did this happen," Albert said. "Three times the demons did that to me. The second time, I was in the state park near Tyler. I tied a hammock in the trees. The sun set, and I was in my hammock. Connie and Johnny (his two children) were in the tent. Jo and Glenn (friends who had brought Albert and his two children to the park) were also in the tent. They had taken us to the park. Everybody was asleep in the tent. Just me in the hammock, in the trees, in the woods. You know me. That's my thing. I go to sleep, and they return. Ugly, ugly-looking things. All around. All around me. Not physical, but in the form of the spirit. One came from my toe, and grabbed me by the neck. I feel like a ton of pressure, choking me, squeezing so hard.

"Jo and Glenn, they are very sensitive. They heard me choking, heard my last breath. They later on shared that they prayed for me in the tent. The last thing I think is, *Oh, I'm done. I'm dead.* My toe was shaking, like the tail of the rattlesnake. That was the last breath that I have. It was too much for me to handle. And again, the Lord of Hosts. Right there! And it was all gone.

"I think, *He keeps reminding me, for me to stop trying to earn my own way.* I still have the old ways, of trying to get my theory, my form of dealing with the spiritual aspects. It was the old me trying to play that role.

"I learned that when you say the Name of the Lord, don't say it in a religious way. Say the Name of the Lord and expect that things are going to happen. If you say the Name of the Lord, expect something to happen. If you want to cast out demons, say the Name of the Lord and expect them to be gone. Practice that. That is what I was learning."

Albert's brother, Sarindy, had also survived the Khmer Rouge and had also come to Texas. He was living in Houston, at the time. Sarindy was experiencing his own version of spiritual challenges, but ones much different from Albert's.

"The last time," Albert continued with his story, "I got a phone call from my brother, Sarindy. He said that there was a huge owl flying around his home at Houston, and the owl said to him that he is to go back to Cambodia, to the jungle. Can you imagine? A night owl, in Houston, calling him and telling him to go back to the jungle. That is so funny. That is the thing. When you are in tune with the darkness—the darkness is also a spirit; I understand now what the 'Fallen Angel' means, and I also understand the term 'Legions.' And that is what happened in Cambodia. The more I go into the scripture, I think, *Oh, my goodness. It all happened in Cambodia.* That is the thing that I understand."

Albert was referring to the story from the Gospel of Luke (8:27) in which Jesus had encountered a man possessed by demons, and had commanded the unclean spirits to come out of the man. Jesus then asked the spirit, "What is your name?" And the spirit replied, "Legion, for we are many." That is what Albert was recognizing about his country: the unclean spirits were "legion," the term for a division of the Roman army usually comprising 3,000 to 6,000 men.

"Anyway," Albert continued, "Sarindy got a call to go back to the jungle, and that was at Christmas time. Can you imagine, he went over and became a monk. Wears the red cloth, shaves his head, pursuing all of that. I got a phone call from him. 'Merry Christmas, Bong.' Can you believe that? He calls me from the mountain jungle in Cambodia, wishing me a Merry Christmas. I think, *Oh well, a monk wishing me a Merry Christmas. How about that?*

"He shared with me that he got in a fight with his Master (high-level Buddhist monk), on the mountain. And this mountain is where not even the Khmer Rouge would go. Average people don't want to go to that mountain. It is a dangerous place. Tigers. Cobras. No one wants to be there. And that is what you do when you follow what Buddhism teaches—you commit, and follow.

"He says, 'Brother, I have a fight with my Master, and I also have this dream that I want to share with you. I want to fly back.' And I say, 'Okay, if you come I will pick you up, and will take you home, and you can share your story here.' And sure enough, he came. But he kept the red cloth, as a monk, and the bald head."

Much of this story is difficult for Westerners to grasp—whether it is the idea of listening to an owl tell you to leave your home to go to the jungles of Cambodia and become a monk, or whether it is being willing to fly half-way around the world to share your concerns with your brother. In Cambodian culture, much emphasis is placed on the respect of younger children for not only their parents, but for their older siblings, as well. Albert was Sarindy's older brother, and Sarindy had great respect for him. Enough so, that he felt the need to return to talk with him for guidance. Albert picked him up at the Dallas/Fort Worth Airport.

"He walked in," Albert said, "and I said to him, 'Brother, I am going to ask you: I am going to anoint you. Is that okay? I am going to anoint you, and pray. Is that okay?' Because, it is our culture that we have such great respect, and because I am older I have an advantage over the younger one. And he says, 'Please do so, if you will.' So I did. I prayed for him. I didn't realize, when I put that oil on him, it would anger evil spirits.

"Then, he shared his dream that was in his head. He couldn't interpret the dream. There were two fish, in his hands. And he also shared how he got in the fight with his Master. My brother, he has such a heart for the truth. He said he told the Master, 'You express your own holiness. You are my Master. But if anything gets on your nerves, you cuss just like the street people.' And the Master says, 'How dare you say such a thing to me?' So I say to him, 'Look at you, you can't even handle my words, without this incredible anger, and all that. And you consider yourself this holy one? Look at you, the words that come out of your mouth, how you cuss at all the people.'

"Then, they get in this big fight," Albert continued. "My brother had to leave the mountain, cross the jungle and go back to the city. And then I interpret the dream to him. I say, 'The fish, that means it is a blessing to us. The fish express our Christian faith. Our Lord, from the first day, got the fishermen to go with Him, and

He fed the people with the fish.' It is our culture that we take the dream seriously, what is in our head, and how it relates to our perspective. I shared with him what a good thing it is that he brings that dream to share with me. 'That fish is for me,' I told him.

"The thing is, my brother, he too had an incredible vision. Before Pross and I went to Kampong Speu (described in a later chapter) Sarindy had already seen me there, in his mind. So he, too, is dealing with the spiritual journey, and someday I hope his heart will be open to the Spirit of God, so he can understand Him more. Because there is something about him, too, even though he wears the red cloth, and is the monk. He sees things that just don't make sense."

"Sarindy said, 'We are in the position of helping the people, but the monks, instead of helping the people, they stand there collecting the money from the people and build a temple. It don't make sense. People are starving in the village.' The monks had built this huge gate, this golden gate. When he saw the gate, he just stood there, weeping and crying so hard. He said, 'It just doesn't make sense. The people are starving, and they build this thing.' So he walked back to his mountain. Later on, he came back to the village, and the gate? Collapsed. Fell down. He believed it was a miracle.

"One other thing. He said one time when he was in the woods, on the mountain, he was having such a spiritual battle. He told me he said, 'If You are the true God, show me. Show me! Do something. Whoever You are, show me. Make it rain.' It was summertime and very hot, and he was still wearing all the red cloth, and all that. All of a sudden, just boooooosh, pours down rain. He was just in shock. He walked out, and there was no rain on the other side. No rain.

"Back to that night he shared the dream. I told him, 'You are my brother. I have great respect for you. I share my bed for you.' So he slept in my bed, and I slept on my couch. That night, that same stuff come back, ugly-looking shapes, on my throat, like over in the state park. The same thing, choking me, to the point of death. When they take my breath, I think, *I'm done, this time.* But the thing they don't realize is that what they are dealing with is the One who is in me. His name is Blessed. I say His Name. Somehow, Satan, they recognize, they understand more than we humans do. Even though He is in us, somehow we humans have lost the connection that is to Him. But the Darkness—they knew, they knew.

"You remember the story in the Bible, when Jesus crossed the sea and came to the man possessed with a demon (Luke 8: 26-28)? When the man fell, the demon said to Jesus, 'I know who You are. I know who You are.' When you are dealing with the spiritual aspect—they know, they know. And that is very important. And at His Name, they left me. And the number is important, too. That was the third time they came, and they never came again.

"I want to share, that the miracle of God is already within us, within our own body. We abuse our body, but it is a miracle. And that is the problem. If we would just live with the miracle of God inside of us, how wonderful it is. You know, what surprises me from all that I go through, I never tell myself to keep on breathing. It was the miracle of God, that we keep on breathing. That breath carry us on in life, keep us moving forward. All the strength, that kept my blood flowing, kept me breathing, kept me alive, was all within me. That is the miracle of God. He creates everything. It is God's holiness, if we don't abuse ourselves.

"With things like the old culture, it is powerful. Very powerful over the mind. But it is not holy. I have to be very careful. Now that I am alive in the Spirit, and look back in the past, I see that if you are not careful, you become like the sheep. It will lead you in the wrong way. When I came out from that, and the Lord began to open my eyes, I tell others to be careful, because you don't know what you are into. You get trapped.

"When I would meditate, I tried to create a self image, a self mentality. I would try to earn from my own being. Now that I am out from that, I meditate not from my own strength, but because of the grace of God. And that grace has helped me to pull out from all of that, because I got so lost in all of that.

"Take my own brother, Sarindy, as an example. He was so in tune in that direction. He surrendered to it, left Houston and went back to the jungle. He tried to seek all that, in the caves and the woods. He was led into another realm of spirit. To me, that is the way of the flesh, how we seek for our own thing. When you've got the Holy Spirit, you can sense the difference. You can see clearly what is spiritual, and what is not spiritual, what is holy and what is not, what is of the flesh and what is of the Lord Jesus Christ."

If Albert was God's "Jonah," to be called to speak out and witness to the people of Cambodia, then Jonah was now ready. His inner struggles were finally gone, he was on fire with the Holy Spirit that had been his sword and shield as he fought his demons, and his spiritual education was advancing at an unbelievable pace. No whale was needed to get him to his Nineveh. His church, Canyon Creek Presbyterian, was to serve that purpose.

Sketch by Albert depicting his battles with his internal demons. The cross symbolizes how Christ restored his wounded heart. This was drawn after his 2005 mission trip where he witnessed to the military.

Mark 8:34 reads, "If any man would come after me, let him deny himself and take up his cross and follow me." This sketch by Albert illustrates his sense of mission, to take the gift of God's Grace that he has received, to his fellow Cambodians.

Section V
Go Into All
The World

Chapter 10

Seek, and You Will Find

Ask, and it will be given you; seek, and you will find; knock, and it will be opened to you.

Matthew 7:7

It would seem that the story was over. Albert Cheng had survived the worst that life could throw at him, had lost his parents, two sisters and a brother, lost his homeland. Yet through it all he had endured and survived, constantly seeking the God that finally, in a blaze of light and glory, found him, and saved him. He could now live a life of peace. Time for the epilogue.

Not at all! Indeed, all that had happened to him proved to be mostly prologue. Now it was time for the "rest of the story." After his conversion and baptism, after the demons were conquered, Albert did not simply sit back and take his new Christian faith for granted. He became a man possessed, not with the demons that had so long haunted him, but instead with a quest for knowledge, seeking answers from every source possible.

"I guess, when you realize how hungry you are, what has been missing from your life for so long, you want to fill up that emptiness as quickly and as fully as you can," Dr. Lewis suggested, when asked about Albert's insatiable hunger for learning. "His faith was not something taken for granted, and when you grow up in another culture, he just wanted to read everything that he could, learn everything that he could, to be a witness."

That quest began, of course, while living with the Browns, listening to John and Marna discuss scripture every morning, asking them an occasional question.

"One of the things that John did that helped Albert a lot was to give him the Navigator memorization plan," Marna Brown said of that quest. "They give you a topic, and a whole long list of verses for each topic that are to be memorized. And where most people really struggle with that, Albert learned every single one of them. He's conversational with every single verse that John gave him, and there are tons and tons of them. He memorized far more of them than John was ever able to do."

Albert's internal struggles with the conflict between his former life as a Buddhist and his new Christian faith had been put behind him. But we are creatures of habit, and old habits are hard to break. Marna Brown was joyful, and grateful for Albert's profession of faith in Christianity, but was concerned about how well he grasped its saving Grace.

"I was afraid that Albert would go from the Buddhist orientation of earning merit," Marna explained, "to a works orientation of salvation. I think there is a fine line on that for most all Christians, especially when one comes out of that kind of background. But I don't really see that in Albert. I see him understanding grace, and all that. He worships night and day, but he worships because he wants to, not because he feels he has to."

Then too, there was Mary Hodge, reading scripture with him, listening to his questions, talking with him. The support of his friend Chheng Nuon, visiting and learning about the scriptures in his native language, was especially meaningful. Now that he had heeded the advice of that friend and dropped all pretense of his old beliefs and practices, he immersed himself in learning his new faith.

For the next year following his baptism in 1998, Albert studied wherever and however he could. Then, in the fall of 1999, the seeds of his new faith received a generous dose of spiritual "Miracle Gro™" when he participated in the Houston Presbyterian Cursillo #8 at Camp Allen, in the beautiful, peaceful isolation of the Texas Piney Woods, an hour's drive northeast of Houston, Texas.

It is hard to imagine two more appropriate contributors to Albert's emotional and spiritual health than for him to be immersed in his new faith, in the woods he so loves. The Piney Woods area of Texas, as the name suggests, is a region of rolling hills luxuriating in pine forests and lakes, stretching along much of the eastern border of the state. It is an area far more akin to the pine forests of the southern states than to the stereotypical Texas desert terrain seen in all the old cowboy movies. From his childhood days in the jungle with Uncle Hank, Albert was always most at home, always most at peace, in the woods. That retreat center deep in the woods, filled with the fragrance of pine and the music of birds chirping, must have made his heart sing.

The Cursillo movement started in Spain not long after the end of World War II, and years later spread to America. The course is described as follows by the Canyon Creek Presbyterian Church website:

> Presbyterian Cursillo is a purposefully designed method for renewing the faith of individuals. "Cursillo" (pronounced Kur-see-yo) means a short course in living the Christian faith and is designed to provide a framework for the development of Christians in the local church and in the world. A Cursillo is a three day weekend retreat filled with

short talks, music, fellowship, small group discussion and joyful experiences.

It was in this experience that Albert was immersed in an ocean of God's love as Cursillistas (pronounced Kur-see-yee-stas)—those who have participated in previous Cursillo weekends—showered first-time participants with gifts of grace. One could easily imagine that driving four hours from home to spend three days with eighty strangers would have intimidated someone not only new to the Christian faith, but still developing his language skills. Overcoming difficulties had long since become part of Albert's life, and he refused to allow those obstacles to impede his search for truth.

The weekend at Camp Allen turned out to be pivotal and transformational. Albert returned home with eighty new brothers and sisters in Christ, a deeper understanding of his new faith, and a hunger for more. The following year, Albert was accepted into The Bethel Series program which was being introduced at Canyon Creek Presbyterian Church. The Bethel Series is a tool which is designed to aid church members in gaining a deeper understanding of the Bible. Its primary objective is to aid students of the Bible in securing an in-depth overview of the scriptures to serve as a base, or a springboard, from which to pursue deeper studies of God's Word.

The Bethel Series came to Canyon Creek Presbyterian through the efforts of a member of the church, George Platt. He, in consultation with Dr. Lewis, and others, selected Mary Hodge to be the "teacher of the teachers." In July, 1999, the two of them attended The Bethel Series training program and in January, 2000, began teaching church members who would become The Bethel Series teachers. Albert was chosen to become one of the teachers. While participating in that two-year Bethel course, Albert took advantage of an opportunity to help others experience God's unconditional love through Cursillo when he served on the staff of North Texas Presbyterian Cursillo #3 in February, 2001. This time the weekend retreat was held at a camp on Lake Lavon, near Richardson, Texas.

It is unlikely at the time that Albert perceived it as such, or was overtly aware of it, but God was preparing him for the mission work to Cambodia that was to come later. As part of this preparation, God put yet another angel in Albert's life. Sharon Wittmann was also a part of The Bethel Series class, and began to assist Albert with the difficult, comprehensive studies.

"I remember after the night that the Lord revealed Himself to me, my miracle experience," Albert said, "I just couldn't grab hold of it all. It was just too much for me to grasp. If I would go to the store, or go out for a walk, I would see everything completely differently. Everything was completely new. I realized, there was a new person inside of me. I didn't know about the Trinity yet, but God's Holy Spirit? Oh my goodness! It was so real.

"I knelt down one night, and I said, 'Lord, for all those many years I went through so much, the suffering, the bloodshed, when I see heads being cut off, the people blown up, my humanity was just gone. I didn't want to see a human anymore, the cruelty, they are just too frightening. But Lord, if I am still able to be useful, then use me.' And from that day on, the pieces of the puzzle began to fall into place. And then I began to get drawn into the Word of God.

"Sometimes I would just read the Word, all night long. Even though I didn't understand it all, when the Word came inside of me and I understood it, I knew it was the Lord, He revealed Himself to me. And I began to see, everything is in the Bible, whether it is good, or bad. It is all in the Bible. And then the Bethel study came along, and Sharon was there to help me.

"I had a vision of the Lord coming into me, coming into the class, teaching me," Albert continued, "and Sharon came into the class. I didn't know her at all. And I didn't know it, but Sharon also had a vision, of Southeast Asia. She didn't know it would turn out to be Cambodia. This is how the Lord puts things together. We became like family, like brother and sister. We didn't realize, this is how the Lord put things together for this mission. When I had my vision, that is when I got baptized. And that is how the Lord worked in His own way.

"At the same time, I was just very hungry for the Word, very hungry, like a dry sponge. Sometimes at night, I would just seek more and more, into the Word. Any other time that I had, any time at all, I would just go off by myself, and seek the Word."

Albert was not alone in experiencing God guiding him toward His mission. As Albert said, Sharon had experienced some guidance of her own, a vision that she was reluctant to share until the time seemed right. When she met Albert, then began to get to know him and his story, the timing began coming together.

"In 1997, a year before I met Albert," Sharon said, "I was praying this same prayer every night. I would pray, 'God, I feel called to do something, but I don't know what You want me to do.' Night after night, I would pray that same prayer, but I didn't feel any response to it. Finally, one night I had a vision. I saw a map of the world. So I said, 'Okay, God, I know You want me to go out into the world, but what do You want me to do?' My focus on the map was on Southeast Asia. I had no connection, then, to Albert or Chheng Nuon, or anybody over there. I had this flood of images, almost like your life passing before your eyes. I said, 'Okay, God, I know You want me to go to Southeast Asia. But not right now, right? My kids are still in school.' I didn't share my vision with anyone. I figured they would think I was crazy. So, I put it aside for a while. Later, when I met Albert, I felt God telling me that my focus was to be on Cambodia."

As Albert had said, all those puzzle pieces were coming together, but as Sharon said in her prayer, "Not right now, right?" There was still much preparation necessary before the mission became clear to all. In the meantime, Albert continued his quest for knowledge.

"One of the things that has impressed me," Marna Brown said of that quest, "is that the Presbyterian church has allowed Albert to grow, and to lead. I think that a lot of churches would not have seen that potential in a custodian. I really admire them, for that. They even sent him down to Austin Seminary, and he's on a national board (National Cambodian Presbyterian Council).

"He said to me, one time, 'You know, Marna, with my finances, I never imagined I would get to travel. And look at me, now. Traveling everywhere. Around the country, back to Cambodia. Can you imagine that?' It's just a God thing, and I really admire the Presbyterian church for helping, for allowing, that to happen."

Indeed, Albert rose to even higher challenges in his new faith with every step forward in his education. The Presbyterian Church (U.S.A.) had been looking for ways to help Southeast Asian congregations enjoy all the advantages of the denomination, including seminary-trained leadership. To meet that need, the Southeast Asian Lay Academy Program was initiated by the General Assembly's Lao Consultant Office to educate key leaders in the basics of Presbyterian doctrine and practice as prescribed for commissioned lay pastors in the Book of Order. The program consists of six core courses taught over the course of three summers: Reformed Theology, Presbyterian Polity, Worship & Sacraments, Bible Interpretation, Teaching in the Reformed Tradition, and Reformed Preaching.

In 2001, Albert was accepted into the three-year Southeast Asian Lay Pastor Training program offered through Austin Presbyterian Theological Seminary. The course involved intensive week-long training each summer, with additional study during the year. Albert completed the course in 2003.

These experiences, whether as student or teacher, were propelling Albert down a road at a pace that must have seemed, at times, a bit overwhelming. But where was that road carrying him? What did it all mean?

In the previous chapter, Albert was likened to Jonah being called by God to go witness to the people of Nineveh. On the surface, all of Albert's training and preparation appeared to be preparing him for such a mission. But where? And for what purpose? Answers to those questions were not immediately apparent, but would soon become so.

Chapter 11

HANDS for Cambodia

Go therefore and make disciples of all nations, baptizing them in the name of the Father and of the Son and of the Holy Spirit...

Matthew 28:19-20

If a brother or sister is ill-clad and in lack of daily food, and one of you says to them, "Go in peace, be warmed and filled," without giving them the things needed for the body, what does it profit? So faith by itself, if it has no works, is dead.

James 2:15-17

And a vision appeared to Paul in the night: a man of Macedonia was standing beseeching him and saying, "Come over to Macedonia and help us."

Acts 16:9

Peggy Lee, a popular female vocalist of the 1950s and 60s, recorded a song in 1969 that rose quickly in popularity. The song, with the title "Is That All There Is?," expresses a rather bleak view of life, a feeling of disillusionment and cynicism. In his early years, that song might have been one that Albert could well have related to. Of course, after his miraculous conversion, his being cleansed of his internal demons, it would have been quite the opposite of how he later came to feel about life. Nevertheless, it posed an interesting question that did relate to Albert. After all that he had endured, after finding his salvation and becoming immersed in the study of the Bible, it did raise the question: "Is that all there is?"

But rather than being an expression of cynicism, in Albert's case the question had an entirely different meaning. What the question meant for Albert was, "What is the purpose of all that has happened to me, and what am I to do about it?" In other words, where Albert's life was concerned, was all that had happened to him "all there is?" Was that to be the end of it? The answer to that question was to turn out to be an unequivocal "No! That is not all there is." Indeed, there was much more to come.

During his three years of dedicated study, Albert had become a student of the Scriptures, a man of the Word. As he studied, delving ever deeper into the teachings of Jesus, two issues emerged. First, one cannot study the New Testament and the teachings of Jesus without quickly coming face to face with the "Great Commission" from the Gospel of Matthew, quoted above. Sermons have been delivered from many pulpits, over many centuries, on Christ's instruction to His Apostles before His ascension into Heaven. His commission to the Apostles, to spread the Good News of the Gospel to all lands, is well known to Christians. And it soon became well known to Albert.

The second issue that presented itself to Albert is what might be called the "Great Dilemma," a way of describing the long-running apparent contradiction regarding salvation: Are we saved by God's Grace? Or by our own works? The seeming conflict posed in the verses from James quoted above has also been the subject of many sermons.

If there were any doubts in Albert's mind about those scriptures, if he sensed a conflict or contradiction, it was not apparent in his actions. He knew what was meant by those teachings, and he knew what he wanted to do about them. As the Great Commission instructed him, he would witness, for the simple but profound reason that he could do nothing else. The Holy Spirit had so filled him that keeping that light under the proverbial bushel was impossible.

Albert clearly understood—and often proclaimed—that he had been saved by the Grace of God, that freely-given gift of redemption that comes from the cross that he now so completely embraced. But just as he could not keep himself from being a witness, he also knew that his faith would be empty if he did not share it with his works, with a life of giving back that which he had received. As emphasized in The Bethel Series, Albert knew that he had been "blessed to be a blessing." He knew what he wanted to do, what he felt he had to do. It seemed it was time for Jonah to head for Nineveh. But how that was to be done was not so clear.

Perhaps it is not obvious, but there is a problem with the Jonah analogy. In that Bible story, Jonah was called—more accurately, forced—to go to Nineveh because of the wickedness of the people. Given the atrocities of the Khmer Rouge, that comparison would not be much of a stretch for Albert. The Khmer Rouge were nothing, if not wicked. And certainly they needed to hear God's admonitions to repent.

However, for Albert and the people of Cambodia a better biblical analogy would seem to be the call from Macedonia (Acts 16:9). As described in Acts, Chapter 9, a Hebrew Pharisee (religious leader) by the name of Saul of Tarsus was zealously persecuting all those who professed to be followers of the crucified Jesus. Religious leaders of the day considered the belief that Jesus of Nazareth was the Messiah to be blasphemy, and any such believers had to be executed.

Saul was a willing practitioner of the persecutions. One day as he traveled to the town of Damascus he was suddenly struck blind by a bright light, and heard a voice saying to him, "Saul, Saul, why do you persecute me?"

In time, Saul was filled with the Holy Spirit and his sight was restored. He became known as Paul, and became the chosen instrument of God to go among the Gentiles (non-Jews) to preach the Gospel. Paul quickly became as zealous at preaching the message of Christ crucified, of salvation by the Grace of God, as he had formerly been zealous at persecuting those same Christians. Much of the New Testament of the Bible is attributed to the man who was later made Saint Paul by the Catholic Church.

Some time after his miraculous conversion, as Paul traveled about preaching the message of Christ to the Gentile nations, he had a vision in which a man from Macedonia pleads with him to come to them, for they were in need of his message. There is much about this story that seems to be apropos to Albert and the people of Cambodia.

The wickedness of the Khmer Rouge notwithstanding, unlike the people of Nineveh, most of the people of Cambodia were not wicked. But they were, like the people of Macedonia, in great distress and in need. They had suffered indescribable treatment. In all probability, it would have been next to impossible to find a living Cambodian at the end of the reign of the Khmer Rouge who had not lost at least one family member during that horrendous time.

Their poverty could hardly be exaggerated, poverty in terms of lack of food, of clean water, of a place to live, of all the fundamental essentials of life. There was virtually no educational system remaining in place, as many schools had been destroyed or turned into prisons, and the teachers systematically executed. The country had been virtually destroyed by the insane policies of the Khmer Rouge leaders under Pol Pot.

There was also great poverty of spirit, and hope. For Albert, two decades, the experience of a miraculous conversion and immersion in an environment of loving and spiritual support were all required before he was able to be free of his demons, to feel that he had emotionally and spiritually survived the horrors of those four years of madness. Most of his fellow Cambodians had none of that to help them heal their emotional wounds, nothing except two decades of on-going grinding poverty.

Just as Paul was called to the people of Macedonia, Albert began to feel called to witness, to share his newfound "Good News." But witness to whom? At first, he began to share his testimony to church audiences now and then, in the Dallas area. Though always cordially received, the people with whom Albert was sharing his story were already confirmed, dedicated Christians. They might listen with great compassion to his story of life under the Khmer Rouge, and express their joy at his conversion, but he was "preaching to the choir." Albert knew in his heart that his real mission, where he was truly needed, was to return to his homeland and witness to the people of Cambodia who were so desperate in their needs. Cambodia obviously should be his "Macedonia."

Easier said than done. Getting to Cambodia is not a simple thing. There are legalities involved, passports, visas, government permissions, and so forth. And airfare to fly half way around the world isn't inexpensive. In a previous chapter it was told of how, in 1996, Albert had become so homesick, and anxious to learn more of the fate of his family, that he was desperate to return to Cambodia. Various friends had assisted him, and he had been able to return to his homeland for a brief visit.

Returning to Cambodia to witness to his belief in the Good News would be a more daunting task than simply managing to go on a personal visit. If he were to be effective, he would need support from some Christian agency. Logistical support, financing and the support of in-country church networks would be essential, if there were to be any hope of success. Albert needed help, and as always when Albert needed help God put an angel in his path to provide that help. But this time, it was more like the story of Christmas, when a host of angels appeared to the shepherds. Albert's "host of angels" turned out to be his fellow church members at Canyon Creek Presbyterian.

If Albert was being prepared, and called, to return as a witness to Cambodia, he was not alone. His influence on the members and life of Canyon Creek Presbyterian Church was growing, as more people came to know him and hear his testimony. In particular, his association with The Bethel Series classes was beginning to influence members of the Mission Committee of the church. That committee, with Sharon Wittmann as Moderator, was responsible for the mission work supported by the church, and was becoming increasingly drawn toward Cambodia because of Albert's life and testimony.

Bit by bit, piece by piece the puzzle was being filled in, the picture of mission becoming more clear. Chheng Nuon, the Cambodian friend who had been so helpful in Albert's searching, in 1999 had given up his comfortable life in America and returned to Cambodia to start a new church over there.

"It was just so amazing, what God was doing," Albert said of the time. "Chheng didn't tell me until later, but that night (the night after he suggested that Albert 'burn the Buddha') he said God called him to sell his house and go back to Cambodia to start a church. He said he kneeled down to pray, 'Okay, God, You want me to go? Send someone to buy the house.' He put the house up for sale, and a week later, someone bought the house.

"I didn't understand it all, but Chheng needed to establish a church. So we went to Dr. Lewis (pastor at Canyon Creek Presbyterian) and talked about it. But at that time our church couldn't support him. That is when a small church in Parker, Texas (a small town on the outskirts of metropolitan Dallas), said they would support him. So that is when he left for Cambodia and started sharing the Gospel, under the tree, in the thatch house. He started a church in the home of his wife's sister."

Albert later became aware that his friend needed Bibles in the Khmer language for his new church. He told Sharon about the need. Sharon was assisting the Vacation Bible School staff and was looking for a mission to support with the offertory money that the children traditionally contributed as part of the VBS experience.

She quickly agreed this would be a marvelous use of the children's Bible School money. That mission was introduced to the children, all of whom loved Albert from his day-care interactions—and escapades—with them. They enthusiastically contributed their offerings each day. At the end of the week over one thousand dollars had been collected, at that time the largest VBS offering ever contributed at the church. Arrangements were soon made for the purchase of Khmer Bibles for pastor Chheng Nuon and his church.

Remembering her own vision, this experience began to lead Sharon to consider other mission efforts for Canyon Creek Presbyterian. Between Sharon's influence as Moderator, and Albert's influence within the church, the Mission Committee began seriously considering how the church might begin sharing the Gospel with the people of Cambodia. Seeking more knowledgeable guidance, the committee turned to the national Presbyterian Church (U.S.A.) to avail itself of whatever resources and guidance might be available.

Watershed changes were occurring at this time in the way so-called "missionary" work was being approached by individual Presbyterian congregations. Previous generations left such work to the official institution. Donations from a congregation would be sent up the ladder to the General Assembly, the official governing body of the Presbyterian Church (U.S.A.), to use as it saw fit.

But now, congregations were finding it far more satisfying—and helpful to the people being served—to become more personally involved rather than simply writing a check to some distant organization. Simply put, today's generation wanted to be directly involved in people's lives, to share in ministry first hand. Rather than looking to the official institution, congregations around the US were beginning to strike out on their own as what has become known as "Mission Initiators."

In due course, the committee learned of the Presbyterian Frontier Fellowship (PFF). Although an independent organization, the PFF works closely with the Worldwide Ministries Division of the PC(USA) to connect individual congregations to people and needs in particular parts of the world. In 2001, a conference of the PFF was held in Cincinnati, Ohio. Albert and Sharon were designated to attend the conference as representatives from Canyon Creek Presbyterian Church.

Albert had not mentioned it to anyone, but he had always assumed that he was the only Cambodian Presbyterian in the country. Imagine his surprise, and joy, when he walked into the conference hall and saw delegations representing countries from all over the world—including Cambodia.

"The day I walked into that conference room, I was overwhelmed to see tables with flags from all different countries from around the world," exclaimed Albert about the experience. "I couldn't believe my eyes when I saw a table with the Cambodian flag on it. I had no idea that there were other Cambodian Presbyterians.

"I was inspired from that meeting and was still in flames," Albert later said of the conference. "I was asking God to lead us in doing God's will for the people of Cambodia."

He and Sharon returned to Canyon Creek Presbyterian Church with a clearer vision for service. Their testimony regarding the conference to the Session, which is the official ruling body of each Presbyterian church, was pivotal. On August 21, 2001 the Session voted to establish as official church policy the commitment of Canyon Creek Presbyterian Church to the people of Cambodia, and approved a resolution, "Commitment to Share the Good News with the People of Cambodia."

Soon after that, Sharon and Albert began teaching The Bethel Series, a two-year Bible study, to members of the Cambodian United Methodist Church and the Cambodian Church of Christ. Later, the Mission Committee of the church began developing a plan for a Vision Quest, a journey to Cambodia to investigate how Canyon Creek Presbyterian Church (CCPC) could best begin to partner with local churches there, such as Chheng Nuon's, to advance God's Word.

The Reverend Pat Beltzer joined the staff at CCPC at about this time, responsible for mission ministry. It took not long for her to join Albert's "host of angels," as she and Sharon began to work together. Sharon decided the time had come to share her vision of being led to Southeast Asia, and told Pat about having been called to go to that part of the world. Of course, by now she had developed a close bond with Albert, which narrowed her vision to Cambodia. They were also working closely with Mary Hodge on their plans.

"Albert introduced us to Chheng Nuon," Mary related, "which narrowed our focus to a specific location. It seemed God was calling us to Cambodia. Several of us began praying about that, and began planning an exploratory trip to find out more about the mission and to try to validate Chheng's ministry. He wasn't Presbyterian; in truth, he wasn't officially affiliated with any denomination. We felt if we were going to ask the CCPC Session to support that church, we had to be able to vouch for Chheng's ministry, its financial accountability, and all the rest.

"So a team came together," Mary continued, "with Albert and Sharon, Pat Beltzer and myself. By then, another new minister, Lee Wyatt, had come to the staff and his wife, Carolyn, had been a missionary to Bangladesh. Carolyn had a heart for mission, and joined the team. George Platt, who had brought The Bethel Series to the church and knew Albert, also agreed to go with us."

It was finally time for Albert to do as the Apostle Paul had done, and "Come over to Macedonia, and help us." Except this time, of course, it wasn't to be Macedonia. January, 2003, in a symbolic book-end to his life, found Albert on board a flight to Bangkok enroute to Phnom Penh. Two decades earlier he had been on the reverse of that flight, enroute from Bangkok to America. At that time, his frame of mind—to the extent that his mind functioned at all—was bent on seeking revenge on all who had so destroyed him and his country.

But Albert was not armed with an AK-47, nor was he seeking revenge. Armed instead with a Bible and the love of God, he was now a member of the Vision group, along with Sharon Wittmann, Mary Hodge and the three other church members enroute to meet with Chheng Nuon and other Christians in Cambodia to seek out the best ways to support those embryonic churches. The Vision group candidly admitted that they had no real idea what they would find or be able to do once they got to Cambodia, so had an open agenda. They all shared a conviction that they were following where God was leading them, and had faith that they would receive guidance once they got there.

The group was met at the Phnom Penh airport by Albert's youngest brother, Doctor Pross, and stayed at his house. During their stay there the group sang, and even attempted to dance traditional Khmer dances with Doctor Pross and his family. The group also shared their Christian faith with their hosts. Albert had been attempting to share that message with his younger brother for two years, and was ecstatic when he and his family all accepted Christ while they were there.

In many respects, the group was not prepared for what they were to encounter once they arrived in Phnom Penh. Poverty, as it exists in a country such as Cambodia, can not be imagined by those of us raised in America—it has to be witnessed to be comprehended. Of course, learning the "lay of the land" was a fundamental goal of the mission trip, and learn they did. The excerpts included below from the report by group member Sharon Wittmann back to the Session of CCPC upon their return made clear that they harbored no illusions regarding Cambodia:

> After the Khmer Rouge was driven from power and the people tried to return to their homes, they often found others living on their land. Those who were lucky to have their homes left intact and their fields not covered with landmines still had to start their lives over with little or no possessions...

There are few paved highways, and most are in poor condition. Clean drinking water is not readily available. Most people, even in Phnom Penh, get their water from a river and have to boil it to make it clean enough to drink. Some who can afford it have wells. Most have large concrete cisterns that collect rain water to store it for future use...

When you see poverty like this, there is an immediate urge to want to help. Coming from our country, which is extravagantly rich by comparison, there is the temptation for us to think that we can fix all of their problems by giving them food, clothing, and shelter, and by building roads and schools and hospitals. While all of these things are well intentioned, over the years we have learned that if you give a man a fish, he can eat for a day, but if you teach him to fish, he can feed himself for a lifetime. When we went to Cambodia, we went as guests and as brothers and sisters in Christ. We didn't go to see what we could **do for** the Cambodian people, we went to see how we could **work with** the Cambodian people in partnership.

That lesson, of not only becoming aware of the overwhelming needs of the country but also that the people of Cambodia could best be helped by outside groups only by working with them—rather than by doing for them—was in itself sufficient justification for the trip. But that was not all that came out of the journey.

Shortly after arriving in Phnom Penh, the group met with Mr. Heng Cheng, the Secretary General of the Evangelical Fellowship of Cambodia, which can best be compared to the National Council of Churches in America. While they were explaining their mission, and their trip to Cambodia, to Mr. Cheng, he gave them a list of Christian groups already in place in the country. To the surprise of the group, they saw on that list the KPF, the Khmer Presbyterian Fellowship of Cambodia. The group was completely unaware of any Presbyterian group functioning in the country.

The explanation, they soon learned, was that Presbyterianism was brought to Cambodia by Presbyterians from South Korea. Decades earlier, Presbyterian missionaries from the United States established churches in South Korea. Those churches had then followed the instruction of Jesus to "Go into all the world" (Mark 16:15), and had sent missionaries to Cambodia.

Founded by an energetic, enthusiastic Cambodian Christian, the organization had already formed soccer teams for youth, a Khmer literacy class so people could learn to read the Bible, and had translated the Presbyterian Westminster Catechism into Khmer. He also was pastor of several new churches. To the Vision group, meeting this dynamic Christian leader was literally a God-send.

Perhaps the single-most valuable consequence of the Vision Quest mission was that the group received, first hand, an unfiltered view of the challenge and opportunity that is Cambodia. As they drove through the streets of Phnom Penh, the abject poverty of the people was stark and unavoidable. Beggars, both children and adults, lined city streets. Many had lost limbs from land mine explosions. People squatted around open fires, cooking food for sale.

Pat Beltzer, who was then an Associate Pastor at Canyon Creek Presbyterian and designated scribe for the mission trip, reported their drive from Phnom Penh to attend worship at Chheng Nuon's church at Prak Ambel:

> We experienced our first ride on Cambodian roads. It wasn't very pleasant! No one could have prepared us for the experience. They weren't really roads, they were more like mountain trails that were filled with cracks the size of ditches... .

As I looked out over this beauty, the best of Cambodia I'd seen so far, I couldn't help but think about the poverty we had seen in Phnom Penh. I will never forget those sad sights: adults and children begging; people with limbs torn off their bodies from land mine accidents; the ugliness of litter and trash; children who lived day to day without food and baths and little clothing; children who lived without the opportunity to attend school, but doing anything they could to help their family survive. Even on the drive down, the rural scenes were just as sad: tiny houses with thatched roofs on stilts in varying stages of ruin; farmers and families trying to make a living off of practically nothing, spear fishing in muddy holes outside their homes; people gathering grasses and sticks, working in the rice fields, water buffaloes here and there wading in the same dirty ponds where little children bathed.

Both churches served by Chheng Noun were visited by the Vision group, which had purchased more Bibles and supplies for Chheng's churches. The group also gave witness and testimony to the many Cambodians who attended the services. As he participated in those services, the profound contrast could not have been lost on Albert.

As related in earlier chapters, virtually all Christians in Cambodia at the time of the fall of Phnom Penh had been killed by the Khmer Rouge, as had many of the Buddhist monks. Churches and temples alike had been destroyed. Under the Khmer Rouge, overt worship in any form was tantamount to committing suicide. To now be able to experience his fellow countrymen freely and openly not just worshipping, but sharing his own new-found God, celebrating with him the Holy Spirit through song and praise, must have been overpowering.

After the fall of the Khmer Rouge regime, Christianity had been approved as a legal religion in Cambodia in 1990. Prior to that, numerous clandestine "house churches" were meeting in secret, and those churches soon came out into the open. Cynics could accuse the move as self-serving, in that it allowed historically-charitable groups into a country needing all the help it could get. But whether the result of magnanimity or cynicism, it permitted Cambodians to openly and publicly accept and practice the Christian faith.

There appeared to be a hunger on the part of many Cambodians, as Albert had so long experienced, for something that offered more hope for their lives than many had found through their old culture. Nevertheless, that culture had existed for more than twenty centuries and was part of modern Cambodian culture in the way that red is part of a rose.

The issue facing the Vision group, and that faces any and all groups attempting to present the Christian message to Cambodia, is how to do that in the context of an indigenous culture antithetical to it in so many ways. The group quickly recognized that the Christian message would not carry any weight, nor have any credibility, if offered in a vacuum and failed to recognize the grinding poverty of the population. Food sufficient for reasonable health, clean water supplies, medical attention, literacy, all were immediate needs.

The issue—or contradiction, in a sense—was forcibly stated in the Book of James in the Bible, as quoted at the beginning of this chapter. Any person proclaiming that there is a loving God who offers the Bread of Life, but ignores the empty stomachs of the people to whom he is witnessing, any person who preaches that Jesus tells us "I am the Living Water" while ignoring the fact that the only drinking water available is a muddy hole, any person who claims that God will heal the sick while ignoring the open sores on a child's back—such a person would be an empty vessel, a "witness" speaking to an empty room.

Sharon Wittmann spoke to that concern.

"Christianity has had a troubled history in Cambodia. A small number of Christian cell churches had been developing and growing in Cambodia, before the Khmer Rouge took over. Of course, the majority of them were killed. Not until 1990 did the Cambodian government declare that Christianity was a legal religion and those underground "house" churches that had been operating clandestinely come out into the open.

"People knew nothing about Christianity, and were suspicious of it. In Kampong Speu, where Pastor Sarourn Soun of the Khmer Presbyterian Fellowship wanted to start a church, the people of the village started meeting in a grass, or thatch-covered, house. They put a little cross on the top of the house, and started a Christian church. That year there was a bad drought. The country was very dry, and people didn't have enough food. The villagers became very angry, and said, 'It is your new God that caused the drought. You brought this new God into the village, and that is what caused the drought across the whole land.' So they burned down the church. But the Christian people in the village didn't get angry. They just built a new grass church. And God's Spirit must have moved the people, because they began to feel God's love. They didn't burn down the new church.

"At that time, we knew nothing about Sarourn, or the church at Kampong Speu. When we were in Cambodia on the Vision mission in 2003, we met the leaders of the South Korean Presbyterian Fellowship when we were in Phnom Penh. They were sponsoring a cell church in Kampong Speu, they told us. And that is how we came to meet Sarourn and learn about his church. In 2004 we conducted a medical clinic at his church.

"Since the burning of his church, God continued to bless them, and they built a new concrete church building, right next to the grass one. But they kept the grass one to remember. That village has been blessed and has grown from zero percent Christian to ninety percent Christian."

Albert had several emotional and especially meaningful experiences while on that and subsequent trips, as might be expected. One in particular stood out.

"What I see over there is the Spirit of God alive all over the place," Albert said. "Demons are being cast out, people healed. God is at work. I am so excited to see that Cambodians are becoming Christians. After all our darkness, I can hardly believe it. One evening, [on the 2004 mission trip] we had to leave the village. We couldn't stay overnight, so we packed up to leave. But before we left, I went out into the evening, all by myself. I met this young man.

"I said to him, 'Nephew'—that's our culture, how we speak. 'How did you come to believe this new God, called Jesus. How do you believe?' He turned to me, and he said, 'Uncle. Because I was dead. And now I live.' I thought, *Hmm. How did he get all these religious answers?* Then he unbuttoned his shirt, and showed me. 'I was stabbed to death. Somehow, I heard the Name of the Lord. Someone breathed that in my ear. And that is how I lived.' When I saw his chest, it blew my mind. I saw Jesus, right in front of me, and the tears just started rolling down. It turned out, it was Pastor Sarourn who prayed for him, at the point of death. And to this day, that young man is a disciple of Sarourn. I see all of that, going on in my country."

Perhaps the best summary of the consequences and benefits of the Vision trip was included in the concluding paragraph of the report to the church Session by Sharon Wittmann:

> Through the Holy Spirit, we immediately felt a connection and bond with our brothers and sisters in Christ.

They were eager to hear what we had to say, and they were very appreciative that we traveled half way around the world to visit them. It meant a lot to them that we genuinely cared about them and their church and were interested in becoming involved in their ministry. I believe that our trip gave them a feeling of being a part of God's universal Church, not isolated in Cambodia, but members of the Body of Christ and His extended Church family.

After the Vision group returned from their exploratory trip and presented its reports, a Cambodia Mission Team was created to develop a mission plan for the church. That plan, to establish a partnership covenant with the Khmer Presbyterian Fellowship, and with Chheng Nuon's Church of Mercy at Prak Ambel, was adopted by the CCPC Session in April, 2003.

In the fall of 2004, another mission team went to Cambodia. This time the group included several of the original team, as well as some from other Presbyterian churches. Several in the group had medical backgrounds. They planned on this trip to do medical clinics at a few select locations. Pastor Sarourn took them to the village of Kampong Speu. They had not been there before, and were so overwhelmed with the poverty of the village that they felt God was calling them to get funding to build a clinic in the village.

Later on, they were discussing their experiences with some officials of Church World Service in Phnom Penh, and related their feelings of being called to establish a permanent clinic in Kampong Speu. They were told by the officials, "The best thing you can do to help these folks is to go back to the US and form a non-profit organization and then come back into the country that way."

The group came back to the States and followed the advice given them, creating HANDS for Cambodia, a 501(c)(3) not-for-profit organization. The acronym in the name stands for Health And Neighborhood Development Services. Sharon Wittmann did most of the research and filled out the application to get it approved by the US government. After it was approved, the group made arrangements with Dr. Pross, Albert's brother in Phnom Penh, to support clinics in Kampong Speu through Pastor Sarourn and the Khmer Presbyterian Fellowship. As they were able to raise money and get it to Dr. Pross, he would buy medicine and supplies and go out to do a clinic.

In June 2009, a HANDS for Cambodia team invited by Pastor Sarourn and led by Albert Cheng and Dr. Pross conducted a medical clinic at Sarourn's church in Kampong Speu. Albert was aware of the church's history and how the original structure had been burned down years earlier. He even knew that the perpetrator would sometimes come to the rebuilt church bringing an axe or huge knife with the intent of harming the Christians. He also knew that even Pastor Sarourn felt threatened by this violent man. Imagine his trepidation when this enemy of the church approached the church building where the clinic was being held and asked for the pastor. Pastor Sarourn wondered, *What does he want? What is he going to do?*

To everyone's amazement, the man had come to confess his sin to Pastor Sarourn. After years of observing how the Christians of Kampong Speu loved one another and cared for each other, he wanted to accept the Living Lord Jesus as his Lord and Savior.

"Pastor Sarourn and I were overwhelmed with his testimony right in front of us," said Albert Cheng, of the experience.

"Pastor Sarourn knew the man could be very violent," Albert wrote in a report to HANDS' supporters, "and to see that God had brought him face to face right in front of the two of us was awesome. At that moment, Sarourn almost had a heart attack! I, too, was overwhelmed by his testimony, and fumbled to operate a voice recorder, camcorder, and a camera to capture this miracle.

Saints, please do know that this is the power of our Living God, and it was such an honor for me to serve Him and you. To God be all the glory forever and ever! Amen."

Pastor Sarourn would later that year write to HANDS with news that the man was continuing to grow in his faith and that his wife was serving on the church's evangelism team, sharing the Gospel of Jesus Christ with other villages. Such is the transforming power of the love of God in Jesus Christ.

Prior to the initial Vision trip in 2003, Sharon Wittmann had been searching for Presbyterian connections in Cambodia and came into contact with the Reverend Paul Friesen, an employee of the PC(USA) World Missions board. Reverend Friesen has liaison responsibility for what the PC(USA) is doing in Laos, Cambodia and Vietnam. There is presently no official PC(USA) organization in Cambodia, working instead with partners such as the Khmer Presbyterian Fellowship.

For a period of time, the South Korean Presbyterian Fellowship had fully funded Pastor Sarourn's church, including his salary. Cultural differences eventually led to that relationship being discontinued, and Reverend Friesen is now trying to help the Khmer Presbyterian Fellowship to adapt the United States model, in which the local church supports itself. That is an enormous change from where the South Koreans paid for the pastor, car, and expenses, to the US model where it is expected that the church members support their own pastor and church. The PC(USA) has provided emergency support for the village and paid for a fresh-water well to be dug at the church, as well as helping with food during a drought. But the ultimate goal is to develop a sense of independence and self-sufficiency on the part of the church members.

"My personal conviction," said Reverend Friesen, "is that the community of believers, Christ's followers, are God's agents of transforming families and social systems, so that as we respond to the offer that Christ gave us of His Kingdom being available to anyone who would enter in, that begins a transformation process within us. And as we enter into our community, it becomes a process of transformation within the community, and that community becomes a transforming agent within the social system.

"Therefore, as we begin to bring the Good News to the sick, the uneducated, those who lack opportunities, in the Name of Christ for the establishment of His Church, you wed the church to community development. I think that is what God would want us to do. That's why I am excited about this partnership of HANDS and Khmer Presbyterian Fellowship. It goes beyond what other NGOs (non-governmental organization) try to do. Other NGOs do a lot of fine work, but how closely does it tie community development with the Gospel, and church development?

"Kampong Speu is one of the best models where I've seen that actually work. The Evangelical Fellowship of Cambodia has a relief and development arm. They were digging some wells, they were doing different kinds of development projects, but Sarourn and his wife and his team went in and invested themselves in literacy, and teaching the Christian faith to people who couldn't read or write, as well as doing projects like clean water, a fish pond or a rice bank. Out of that, a church has been born that has transformed the way people think about their life, about their destiny in life. Whatever fate they might have thought was ruling their life has been replaced by hope."

As an example of the change in thinking that Reverend Friesen is trying to encourage involves the medical clinic for Kampong Speu. Where the group had originally intended to establish a permanent clinic facility for the village, Mr. Friesen is helping them take a step back and ask, "Is that the best thing for the village?"

"Our recommended approach," Friesen states, "is for the KPF to meet with the village leaders, and get them to agree that the village needs a clinic—then ask themselves how they can accomplish that goal. Villagers may not be at a point where they know how to do such things, but will be better off in the long term if they develop such self-sufficiency. HANDS, and groups like that, can be of enormous benefit in that process."

One proven strategy for doing that is CHE, or Community Health Education. CHE is a multi-faceted, community-based development strategy that deals with the whole person—physically, spiritually, emotionally and socially. Its leaders train people to know how to best go into a village that has never had clean water, never had a sense of proper hygiene and how it relates to good health, and show the people why that is important and how to do it.

Reverend Friesen wants the Khmer Presbyterian Fellowship to have its pastors take the training offered by CHE to help the villagers where they have churches. HANDS is committed to funding that training and expects the program to begin in 2010.

HANDS, because it now has a secure means of wiring funds to Cambodia, has become the funnel through which other organizations are sending funds to the country. For example, a church in Lowell, Massachusetts wanted to send money for Khmer Bibles and used HANDS to facilitate that transfer, likewise a church in Birmingham, Alabama that is funding a mobile medical clinic and an adult student enrolled in a Bible school.

An unspoken, but very real, impediment to villager self-sufficiency is the memory and latent fear of the Khmer Rouge. The older villagers well remember the extermination of such leaders. The Khmer Rouge killed known leaders, people like Albert's father—the educated, the skilled, those who would normally be expected to "make things happen." The obvious consequence was a paranoid fear of being identified as a leader, because the villagers identify being a leader with being executed. HANDS, and other organizations, are in essence having to help recreate a new generation of leadership with the local villagers. As in most all things, though, time is helping heal those wounds.

"If you ask anyone to stand up, to be a leader," Albert confirmed of that paranoia, "you will never get anyone to stand up, to do that, because of the fear of execution by the Communist leaders. When I became a Christian, and read the Scriptures that say to go into the culture, into the country, my hope is that, 'Wow, I see the country is coming back to life, because I see Jesus as their leader. I see the women beginning to rise up, and people stand up. People are still sort of afraid, because some of the current leaders are former Khmer Rouge. But they opened up the country to Christianity. Can you imagine that? It is God, doing all that. God is turning all that evil into good."

When Albert Cheng was born, his mother chose the name of Sophanarith for him. Albert explained that in Khmer, the name means "potential," or "power." As all mothers do for a newborn child, she envisioned great things for him, believing her new son would have the potential, the power, to achieve them. There was, of course, no way she could have known it, but she was prescient in ways she could never have imagined.

Albert's mother never got the pleasure of seeing how well she had named her son because she was brutally killed by the Khmer

Rouge. But it was those same Khmer Rouge who, many years later, were to demonstrate how much power her son would exhibit when filled with the Holy Spirit. It was on an August, 2005, mission trip that Albert and his new God got his biggest test.

Many of us, Christian or otherwise, are familiar with the story of the Roman Emperor Nero "fiddling while Rome burned." The disastrous fire of AD 64, that resulted in the destruction of vast areas of Rome, was blamed by Nero on that strange new cult of people calling themselves Christians. To deflect blame from himself, the Christians had to be punished. That deceit led to another iconic story that most of us know, namely the stories of Christians being fed to the lions in the Coliseum, for public entertainment.

It is safe to say that story is a good analogy for the way Albert felt when requested to witness to a group of Cambodian military officers—many of whom were former Khmer Rouge.

"This is my most powerful testimony," Albert said of the day he stood before former persecutors of his country. "God put me out there in the place where I hate it the most. These are all Cambodian military. These people, they kill two, three hundred people. There was one top officer, who really bothered me. Now he and I have become very close friends. That just shows how God opens our hearts."

Albert knew as he walked onto the military base to give his testimony that many of the military that he would be talking to were former Khmer Rouge, the very people who may have been his captors, or who could have killed his family.

"When I walked onto that base," he admitted, "I didn't want to find out much, because I knew my emotions could not handle it. I told the Lord, 'I don't want to see any of those things again.' But I learned later on that God wanted me to face the maturity of my own self, and also to show that the forgiveness of God can flow from within me. I was struggling all the time there, but the comforting comes from the Lord. I felt like God just gave me a big smile."

Albert had another source of comfort that day, as he prepared himself mentally and emotionally for what lay ahead of him. The music of Robin Mark, the well-known and loved composer and singer of Christian music, was a favorite of Albert. And he drew much comfort and strength from Mark's music, that day.

"I love Robin Mark's music so much," Albert said, "and listened to it that day as I walked onto the military base to help prepare me for my testimony to the military men. It helped calm my nerves, and was a God-send."

Thus comforted and strengthened, Albert met with the group, and offered his heart-felt testimony.

"On the last day, I was facing a group of about thirty of them. I told them 'Now that you know who I am, and you know who Jesus is, I am not going to force any of you to do anything.' I said to them, 'If you think that you would want to accept Jesus as your Lord and Savior, the decision is yours alone. You can just raise your hand, if you want to.' And I stepped back. Then this one commander, he raised his hand, and at the same time he pulled his Golden Buddha from inside his shirt. He wore it on a chain around his neck. He said to me, 'You bring this new God to me, what do you want me to do with this?'

"Oh my, I was struggling, I was scared to death. I have to just stand, because anytime, if I don't have the answer, I just listen. I knew that I could not answer that question, because when you are dealing with the evil and the darkness, with the military, you have to think twice. If you don't have anything at all, you just wait, knowing that something is going to happen.

"And then another officer stood. And he said, 'Sir, let me put it this way. Suppose you want to cross to the other side of the Mekong River. And there are two canoes. Do you put one foot on one canoe, and one foot on the other canoe? Do you think you can cross, that way?'

"I knew right away, it was the Spirit of the Lord, He just came right into it, and saved me at that moment. I think, *This is so clever. So clever.* It was just like when the Pharisees were trying to trap the Lord, and He said, 'What is Caesar's, give it to Caesar. What is the Lord's, give it to the Lord' (see Matthew 22:15-22).

"Then, all of a sudden, everybody in the room raised their hand. Everybody. I almost fell flat on my face, I was just so shocked. But I had mentioned the word 'sin,' and they knew what it was. One of them, he came up to me afterward, and he said, 'Do you think when I kill so many people, that this God could forgive me?' Someone else whispered in my ear, 'The commander killed even more. Do you think God can help him?' It was just the Holy Spirit flowing through me that did it all."

Albert is firm in his conviction that the "potential" that his mother saw in him was from the Holy Spirit, that the Holy Spirit was walking with him through all his suffering, and guided him across not just mine fields, but across oceans, through strange new cultures and finally to the cross that changed his life with a bolt of lightning one night in a dream. That same Holy Spirit guided him in his new studies, led him in his new faith, and ultimately brought him back home to lead his countrymen, even those who had so persecuted him, to the God that now strengthened him.

It is a story not even his mother could have imagined, a true story of God's amazing grace—a gift available to all, that God might lead you home.

May the God of hope fill you with all joy and peace in believing, so that by the power of the Holy Spirit you may abound in hope.

Romans 15:13

Chapter 12

The Next Chapter

For I know the plans I have for you, says the Lord, plans for welfare and not for evil, to give you a future and a hope.
Jeremiah 29:11

As a movie comes to a close, a true story based on people's lives and experiences from sometime in the past, we usually want to know how it all worked out. What is the hero doing now? Did he, in fact, get to marry the girl? Because of that curiosity, it is not unusual to see brief commentaries answering those questions, as the credits roll.

So it is with Albert. You might be wondering, for example, what he is doing now. How is life going for him, after all his dramatic and emotional experiences? In an attempt to answer those questions, consider this to be not so much an epilogue as it is "the next chapter," in his life. And that next chapter already has its own share of excitement and new adventures for Albert.

The biggest of those adventures started during a trip to Cambodia in 2004, when his brother, Sarindy, introduced Albert to Thavy Sok. Sarindy knew Thavy because his wife is related to Thavy's godmother, and he believed Albert and Thavy would make a nice couple. Apparently he was right, because during Albert's trip to Cambodia in August, 2005—the trip where he shared the Good News of Jesus Christ with Cambodia's military leaders—he also shared a special ceremony with the beautiful young Cambodian woman—he and Thavy became engaged.

Dr. Pross, the younger brother of Albert and Sarindy, also knew Thavy, her father and her brothers. (Thavy's mother died in 2003.) Soon after Dr. Pross began conducting mobile medical clinics on behalf of HANDS for Cambodia, he invited Thavy to assist with administration duties and to use her skills as a hairstylist for villagers wanting a haircut or needing treatment for head lice.

When the Khmer Rouge marched into Phnom Penh on April 17, 1975, Thavy was just nine months old. Although she doesn't remember details about the horrible years that the Khmer Rouge were in power, she remembers the feelings of growing up surrounded by war and corruption.

"It was very frightening," she said, of those times. "Although the war ended, the corruption continued. There was no such thing as trust. The word meant nothing to me. I saw people who were trustworthy with someone or something, and then they ended up being killed by people they trusted the most.

"One day, Dr. Pross invited me to go to the clinic at Kampong Speu. It was there that I began to observe and learn about the Christian faith. My first trip to this remote village was full of doubt. I had never heard of the Christian faith. On the second trip, my heart was stirring. By the third trip I was overflowing from within, full of joy and peace, because each farmer's face was radiant, regardless of their poverty. The Lord Jesus was indeed coming alive in my inmost being, and my spirit was convicted. I doubted no more. This was the first time in my life that I experienced the true love of Christ Jesus and I was so thankful for His love, love that led Him to die on the cross for me.

"Love was not part of my old religion; only fear and duty. As a Chinese girl, I not only worshipped Buddha, but ancestors. Every day from sunrise to sunset I would offer fruits and food of all sorts. I was in a spiritual battle between my new life in Christ and the old me. Then one night I prayed in the Name of the Lord Jesus Christ and by morning, there was a feeling of peace in my heart. My confusion was gone."

Once Thavy and Albert were engaged, she filed the appropriate legal documents to immigrate to the United States. Later she learned that the file had been lost and she had to file all over again at great cost. Her obstacles did not end there. Once the paperwork was approved, she knew she would have to travel to Bangkok, Thailand, for an interview at the US Embassy. At that time, there was no US Embassy in Cambodia.

For over two years Thavy and Albert only met each other on the phone. She would ride her motorcycle to an internet café in Phnom Penh and use their phone. One day as she was making her way to the internet café, a large commercial truck hit her from behind throwing her into the air. "I smashed onto the concrete," she said, recalling the incident. "When I looked up, the huge truck was on top of my motorcycle, but had missed my head and my body. Without the Grace of God, I wouldn't be alive today."

God's grace continued to flow and on November 27, 2006, her papers were approved by the US Government, but there was still the matter of an official interview.

"On June 29, 2007, while I was talking with Albert at the internet café," she said, "my cell phone began to ring. I answered it and heard the voice saying that I had an appointment to come in for an interview with the US Embassy. I was extremely overjoyed and speechless! Then I realized that Albert was still on the other line asking if I was all right. When he heard my good news, he praised the Name of the Lord Jesus Christ for His mercy and His grace for both of us.

"In the midst of my joy, I was worried about flying to Bangkok for the interview. However, the next day, the US Embassy moved to Phnom Penh! Another miracle! On the day of my interview, there were thirteen candidates. I was number twelve. Only three people that day passed the interview and were accepted to come to America. Another miracle!"

Things were falling into place, yet the path to America still contained hurdles. Thavy needed an airline ticket.

"I couldn't find a ticket anywhere in Phnom Penh!" she lamented. "But, after praying and fasting for my Lord Jesus Christ, I finally got a one-way ticket to come to the United States of America for the first time in my life. Soon I would be reunited with my husband-to-be. I could hardly believe it: God even answered my prayers for an airline ticket! Our God is awesome! In the name of the Lord Jesus Christ, the God of the Universe, there is hope, assurance, peace, joy, love, mercy, and compassion in God the Holy Spirit. Yes, God does have a plan for my life to love Him and to worship Him forever."

Albert was waiting at the Dallas/Fort Worth airport with flowers when his bride finally arrived on Saturday, July 28, 2007. They were married the following Saturday, August 4, at Canyon Creek Presbyterian Church in a small, family ceremony to quickly satisfy US Immigration requirements. Three weeks later, on August 25, they and a host of friends and family gathered at a Cambodian Methodist church in nearby Carrollton to conduct another ceremony, this time with Cambodian flair!

Thavy joined Albert in worship at Canyon Creek Presbyterian Church and was baptized on April 27, 2008. God's grace had led her home.

Like Albert, Thavy longed to help her fellow Cambodians. In June 2009, she, Albert, and Albert's son, Johnny, were sent by HANDS for Cambodia in conjunction with Eastminster Presbyterian Church of Birmingham, Alabama to conduct medical clinics in several villages. They were joined by Albert's niece, Srey Lak, who had been assisting Dr. Pross with the clinics for several years. Srey Lak's mother, Phana—Albert's older sister—was killed by the Khmer Rouge. She and her husband were just two of the medical professionals murdered during that dark time. Light, however, is returning to Cambodia.

A new light is also shining in the Albert Cheng family. On February 26, 2010, Thavy gave birth to their son, Samuel Kosal. In the Old Testament of the Bible, Samuel is the son of Elkanah and his wife, Hannah, who in gratitude for having been blessed with a son dedicated Samuel to God. Samuel grew up to serve God in the temple, under the tutelage of the priest, Eli. Several times one night, God called "Samuel, Samuel." At first, Samuel thought it was Eli calling him. But finally, Samuel answered, "Speak, Lord, for your servant is listening."

In light of Albert's experience, of being found by—called by—God, naming his son "Samuel" would seem to be a gracious "Thank you" to God. The significance of his son's name doesn't end with his first name. His middle name, Kosal, means "the blessed one." With the name of Samuel Kosal—and being born the son of two parents who by their lives answer, "Speak, Lord, for Your servants are listening"—there can be no doubt that God has special plans for this newest gift of Grace.

Albert's childhood home in Pursat. Note the water marks on the tall columns that keep the main floor of the house above water during the monsoon season. (photo by Albert Cheng)

The school in Pursat which Albert attended as a a child. The man standing at the entrance was the principal at the time the picture was taken in 2009. (photo by Albert Cheng)

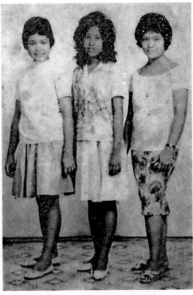

Albert's oldest sister, Phana, on right. (Phana was brutally killed by the Khmer Rouge, as was her husband.) Albert's sister, Ty, on left, is now the oldest sibling. Cousin Kosame is in middle. (photographer unknown)

Albert, with wife Sineth and daughter, Connie, being honored by his employer, The Episcopal Church of the Good Shepherd, upon his becoming an American citizen on April 12, 1989. (photo from Albert Cheng)

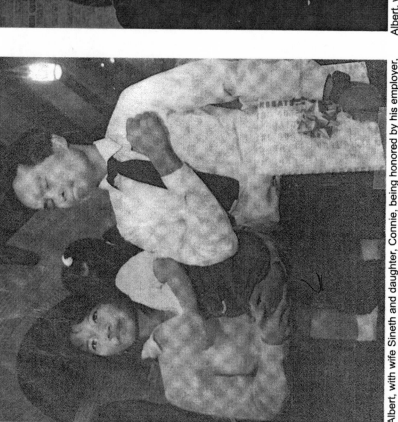

Albert, with Mary Hodge and Dr. Lewis, at Albert's baptism at Canyon Creek Presbyterian Church, February 22, 1998. (photo by John Brown)

Entrance to the historic Angkor Wat temple/city, near the city of Siem Reap. Restored in the 1940s, it has become Cambodia's leading tourist attraction, visited by more than one million tourists annually. (photo by Carolyn Wyatt)

Vision 2003 team at Angkor Wat. From left, George Platt, Carolyn Wyatt, Pat Beltzer, Mary Hodge, Albert Cheng, and Sharon Wittmann. (photo by Dr. Pross)

Albert, with Chheng Nuon and Pat Beltzer at Chheng's church in the remote village of Sre Treng, taken January 2003. (photo by George Platt)

Pastor Sarourn (on right) with the man who burned down Pastor Sarourn's first church in Kampong Speu. The man was inspired by the forgiving nature of the Christian villagers, and became a Christian. He is shown here giving his testimony. (photo by Albert Cheng)

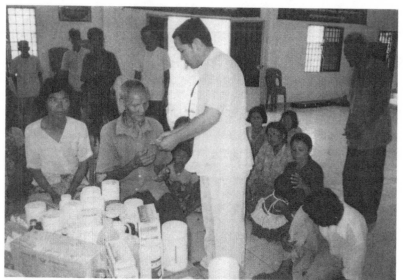

Dr. Pross, conducting a HANDS' medical clinic at the Khmer Presbyterian Fellowship church in Kampong Speu. (photo by Dr. Pross's son, Sandoset)

Albert with (l-r) his niece, Srey Lak, wife Thavy, youngest brother, Dr. Pross, and the Reverend Paul Friesen, prior to conducting a HANDS' medical clinic in Kampong Cham, June 2009. (photo by Johnny Cheng)

Vision 2003 team with Albert's extended family. Albert's sister, Ty, is standing third from left, niece Srey Lak (daughter of oldest sister Phana, who was killed by the Khmer Rouge) fourth from left. His youngest sister, Lin is standing sixth from left and youngest brother, Dr. Pross, is standing at far right. Albert is kneeling, front right. (photo by George Platt)

Albert with his daughter, Connie, and son, Johnny, at his house in Garland, Texas. Photo taken approximately 1998. (photographer unknown)

Albert and Thavy Cheng on their August 25, 2007, wedding day, with Albert's daughter, Connie, and son, Johnny. (photo by Mengly Chean)

Additional Resources

The following books and websites are excellent resources for additional information about the history of Cambodia, Pol Pot and the Khmer Rouge.

Pol Pot; Anatomy of a Nightmare
Written by Philip Short and published in 2004, this is perhaps the most exhaustively researched, comprehensively presented, book available on Pol Pot and the Khmer Rouge. Although the book focuses on Saloth Sar, who later became known as Pol Pot, it is in fact a wide-ranging history of geo-political forces and the people who were most influential in the arena of Cambodian politics during the twentieth century. The book is supported by a vast array of supporting research documents, all carefully annotated.

Killing Fields, Living Fields
This book presents the history of Christianity in Cambodia, from the nineteenth century to modern times. Written by Don Cormack, who spent many years living in Cambodia and writes from first-hand experience. His relating of the fall of Phnom Penh to the Khmer Rouge is especially compelling.

First They Killed My Father; a daughter of cambodia remembers
The first-person story of Loung Ung, a Cambodian girl who, at age five, experienced the fall of Cambodia to the Khmer Rouge. She ultimately survived and made her way to America, and relates all she experienced during those wrenching years.

Imagining America, by Sharon Sloan Fiffer

The story of Paul Thai, another Cambodian survivor of the Khmer Rouge, who came to Dallas, Texas and eventually became a member of the Dallas Police Department.

Golden Bones; An Extraordinary Journey from Hell in Cambodia to a New Life in America, by Sichan Siv

A native of Cambodia, Sichan Siv escaped forced labor camps in 1976 and was resettled as a refugee in Wallingford, Connecticut. He was nominated by President George W. Bush in 2001 and unanimously confirmed by the Senate as a United States Ambassador to the United Nations, serving until 2006.

www.cambodia.org

Everything you might want to know about modern Cambodia.

www.yale.edu/cgp

Website of the Yale University Cambodian Genocide Program.

www.omf.org/omf/cambodia/about_cambodia/buddhism_profile

Summary of history, origins and beliefs of Buddhism.

HANDS for Cambodia
HEALTH AND NEIGHBORHOOD DEVELOPMENT SERVICES

HANDS for Cambodia provides health care, health education, clean water, and community development to those in need in Cambodia. Since 2005 when HANDS for Cambodia was established as a 501(c)(3) not-for-profit organization, it has worked with the Khmer Presbyterian Fellowship (KPF), National Cambodian Presbyterian Council (PCUSA), Church World Service, and other charitable organizations to address the physical, mental, and spiritual health of the people they serve. Each member of the board volunteers his or her time; there are no employees. This means less administrative costs and more money going directly to ministry.

HANDS conducts mobile medical clinics to bring healing and hope to hundreds of villagers without access to medical care. Dr. Nidamony Thong ("Dr. Pross"), who lives in Phnom Penh, is the brother of HANDS' vice president, Albert Cheng. Dr. Pross coordinates these mobile, curative clinics with Khmer Presbyterian Fellowship pastor Sarourn Soun. Albert's niece, Srey Lak, assists Dr. Pross with the necessary administration of each clinic. This allows the doctor more time to treat the hundreds of patients who arrive presenting a range of symptoms including the following: diarrhea, malaria, tuberculosis, rhinitis, otitis media, pneumonia, hypertension, heart failure, vulvovaginitis, cervicitis, diabetes, gangrene, snake bite, Korsakoff's Syndrome, post-traumatic stress disorder, and much more. Each clinic costs approximately $1000, including $700 in medicine, $130 for the doctor and his assistant, and $170 for transportation and administration.

The vision of Pastor Sarourn, Pastor Socheat, and Dr. Pross is to build a three-story medical/education center in which one floor is dedicated to the care of patients, including a comfortable waiting area, restrooms, clean water, sterile examining and operating rooms, and a laboratory. A second floor will provide classrooms and worship space, while the third level will offer living quarters for medical students. Estimated construction cost: $80,000.

Carolyn Wyatt, President and Executive Director of HANDS, expressed the sentiment of the entire board in the 2009 Annual Report to supporters in saying, "We are grateful for those who support this ministry through prayer and through finances. Our vision is to establish a sustainable medical program and because of your undergirding, we are on track to begin implementation of the Community Health Education (CHE) program in 2010. What a wonderful way to celebrate the fifth anniversary of HANDS as together we help transform *killing fields* into *living fields!*"

For more information or to make a secure online credit card contribution using PayPal, please visit the HANDS for Cambodia website at www.handsforcambodia.com or contact Carolyn Wyatt at Carolyn@handsforcambodia.com. To be placed on the email list for periodic updates, or to schedule a HANDS presentation, email Secretary Mary Hodge at mary@handsforcambodia.com.

CPSIA information can be obtained
at www.ICGtesting.com
Printed in the USA
FFOW02n0228051114
8490FF